How To Become A Teenage Millionaire*

HOW TO BECOME A TEENAGE MILLIONAIRE*

TODD TEMPLE
Illustrations by Steve Björkman

OLIVER
NELSON

A Division of Thomas Nelson Publishers
Nashville

To my parents
Cap and Joan Temple

Copyright © 1991 by Todd Temple

Published in Nashville, Tennessee, by Oliver-Nelson Books, a division of Thomas Nelson, Inc., Publishers, and distributed in Canada by Lawson Falle, Ltd., Cambridge, Ontario.

Printed in the United States of America.

Library of Congress Cataloging-in-Publication Data

Temple, Todd, 1958–
    How to become a teenage millionaire : actually, just some great
ideas to help you make, save, and spend money wisely / Todd Temple :
illustrations by Steve Björkman.
        p.   cm.
    Includes bibliographical references.
    Summary: Discusses how to make money, how to keep it, and how to
spend it wisely, examining such aspects of personal finance as jobs,
banking, and credit.
    ISBN 0-8407-9579-3
    1. Teenagers—United States—Finance, Personal—Juvenile
literature.   2. Finance, Personal—Juvenile literature.
[1. Finance, Personal.]   I. Björkman, Steve, ill.   II. Title.
HG179.T4   1991
332.24—dc20   90-26645
                                                        CIP
                                                         AC

2 3 4 5 6 — 96 95 94 93 92 91

CONTENTS

ACKNOWLEDGMENTS

When I decided to write this book, it wasn't because I know all about money and jobs. It's just that I happen to know the phone numbers of a bunch of people who *do*. So I called my big-time business executive associates and financial whiz-kid friends: their ideas and experiences inspired much of the book.

I especially wish to thank George Logan, Allen Smith, Richard Smith, and Steve Torrey for sharing their expertise in investing, money management, credit, accounting, and business. I also want to thank Victor Oliver (publisher), Lila Empson (editor), and Steve Björkman (illustrator) for making all this information readable.

And I want to acknowledge Melissa McKinley and Dennis Alexander, two students who first read the manuscript and showed me where I could make it better. As they suggested, I took out the really boring stuff—including the list of financially unstable savings and loans. This condensed the book a bit from its original 2,098 pages. (I ignored some of their other suggestions because I was afraid they might let it go to their heads and suddenly demand that their names be listed alphabetically on the cover, which would put my name last—which is how it's appeared on the covers of my four previous books because I always choose coauthors with names near the front of the alphabet, and this is my first book by myself, and nobody's going to make me take up the rear, thank you.)

Thank you, Melissa. Thank you, Dennis.

PART ONE

ISN'T BIG ENOUGH TO GET A TITLE

1

THEY WANT YOU

You're a baby boomer's baby. That means your parents were born in the several years after World War II, when having babies was *the* thing to do. They called it a baby boom because the population exploded—we're talking babies everywhere. From 1950 to 1960, the U.S. population grew by 28

million—18.5 percent.[1]* Of course, most of those babies grew up. They dressed funny and listened to oldies music; they met each other, fell in love, got married, and made you and your friends.

And they made a lot of you: over 23 million, last time I counted heads.[2] One out of every ten Americans is a teenager right now. Big deal, right? To some people this is a really big deal—*worth billions of dollars.*

The people who make shoes, hamburgers, movies, and music have got your number, and they're running it through their calculators:

23 million teenagers × 2 pairs of athletic shoes a year × $70 per pair = $3.2 billion
23 million teenagers × 3 fast-food meals a week × 52 weeks × $3 per meal = $10.8 billion
23 million teenagers × 2 movies per month × 12 months × $5 per ticket = $2.8 billion
23 million teenagers × 10 cds a year × $15 per album = $3.5 billion

You're a booming business to them. You buy all these things for yourselves, and you also have a major effect on the stuff your parents buy: food, electronics, vacations, and cars. ("Sure, Mom, we can all fit in a Miata—the twins can ride in the trunk.") In 1989 teenagers spent *$71 billion* on themselves and their families.[3] That means companies can afford to spend millions of dollars to try to get part of that amount.

They Want Your Money

Since you have what they want, they're going to try really hard to get it from you—which means you're going to have to

---

*These little numbers refer to the sources of my information, which are listed in the back of the book (just in case you thought I was making up this stuff).

try even harder to hold onto it. But it's not like you're Bambi and every company out there is a wolf shopping for someone to snack on.

You *are* a consumer: you need shoes, food, and entertainment, and these companies exist to provide you with these things. There's nothing wrong with charging you a fair price for these products—you don't see us *giving away* this book.

Even companies that try to sell you what you don't need for more than you can afford know that if they take too big a bite out of you now, they'll lose you as a customer for the rest of your long life. If they want to stay in business, they'd better treat you right.

And this puts you in a wonderful position: *you can expect and demand quality*. If a company gives you poor merchan-

IN 1989 THE PRESIDENT OF DISNEY, FRANK WELLS, MADE $50,946,000—THAT'S $16,329 PER HOUR (60 HOURS A WEEK × 52 WEEKS).

dise, lousy service, or empty promises, you and your friends can spend your billions of dollars elsewhere. It's a buyer's market.

But most teenagers don't know this. They save too little through poor investments, spend too much on "stuff," and borrow even more at inflated rates; in short, they're walking around like Bambis, and plenty of people out there have a taste for venison.

They Want Your Body

The size of your age group puts you in another good position: the job market. Although 23 million seems like a lot of people, it's actually fewer than the number of teenagers there

were a few years ago. At the same time, more jobs have opened in "service" fields, which are popular with student workers: restaurants, day care, retail stores, health care, and so forth. In other words, there are fewer teenagers than there are teenage jobs.

For some students, the shortage of workers means they can be rude and careless and not get fired (although irritated customers may occasionally punch them in the nose). But if you're willing to work hard, you can make very good money and gain lots of experience.

Good jobs and wages aren't guaranteed. Some parts of the country have few jobs available, so the employers can be picky and the competition for jobs can be fierce! A downturn in the economy can make it even tougher. The ideas in this book can help you find, get, and keep a job, regardless of the job market.

But What Do You Want?

It's nice to be wanted by advertisers and employers. But the reasons they want you usually have to do with their "bottom line"—the last line on a financial sheet that shows how much money they make. What's good for their bottom line isn't always what's best for yours.

What's your bottom line? What's your purpose for living this year? If it's to work hundreds of hours at low wages, you and employers have compatible bottom lines. If it's to spend every penny of your money on albums, the music companies love you. But your bottom line isn't financial. I'll take a wild guess and say that your bottom line includes

- to be free.
- to be happy.

TWENTY-TWO PERCENT OF TEENS STRONGLY INFLUENCE THEIR PARENTS' CAR-BUYING DECISIONS.

- to love and be loved.
- to grow wiser.
- to make a difference in the world by being an asset to your family, friends, community, country, and planet.

What's good for their bottom line isn't always what's best for yours.

One of the ways money can make a mess of your bottom line is by forcing you to grow up too fast. Lots of high-school students race into adulthood by developing expensive habits in clothing, cars, toys, and entertainment—then they work long hours and borrow money to pay for it all. You come home late after work too exhausted to study for an exam; you collapse on your bed and look around the room: a nice ste-

reo, new TV, VCR, phone, twenty-five cds, car keys, and con-
cert tickets on the dresser. And you're miserable. You were
happier playing hide-and-seek and racing Popsicle sticks
down the gutter.

You can't remain a kid forever. But neither can you ever
regain the freedom you have right now to play and learn and
dream so inexpensively. You have to constantly ask the question: What's best for *me?* Not what's best for advertisers. Not
what's best for employers. *What's best for me?*

YOU WERE RIGHT, DAD, MAKING MONEY
IS HARD WORK.

Make money. Save money. Spend money. But don't let
money mess up your bottom line.

You guessed it. This book isn't going to make you a millionaire before your twentieth birthday.* But it *will* help you take the control of your bottom line away from the advertisers, employers, bankers, and lenders, and put it where it belongs—with you. (And all this time you thought "bottom line" was something you get from sitting on bleachers too long.)

---

*If it does, call me to discuss the commission.

PART TWO

IS ABOUT MAKING MONEY

2

TEENAGE JOBS:
FAST LANES AND
DEAD ENDS

So you want to get a job. Before you start applying, decide what you want the job for. I recently interviewed students on tape, asking them why they wanted to find jobs. Here are some of their responses:

"I want to buy a car."

"I'd like to learn more about business."

"Is this thing on?"

"My dad's making me."

"I'm saving for college."

"I want to get some money so I can move out on my own

and get my mom out of my face because she comes into my room and walks on my clothes and screams at me to clean up and go vacuum the house and I can't stand it anymore 'cause she's driving me crazy and she hates my friends . . . says . . . slob . . . how many times . . . floor wax . . . hell . . . freezes . . . [transcription difficult—student seems to be swinging tape recorder around by the cord] so get out . . . nagging . . . didn't do it . . . over my dead . . ." [End of transcript—student threw tape recorder at the wall.]

For whatever reason, over half the teenagers ages sixteen to nineteen (about 8 million) work part-time after school, on weekends, or during the summer.[4] Millions of students ages thirteen to fifteen also work by delivering newspapers, baby-sitting, gardening, cleaning, selling, and performing a thousand other jobs.

TEENAGE JOBS: THE GOOD, THE BAD, AND THE UGLY

If you decide to join the teenage work force, you'll be getting much more than a paycheck for your efforts. A good job can give you great rewards:

• It shapes the way you perceive work. A good experience now will make work in the future better. Since you'll probably be working for the next forty to fifty years of your life, it's nice to start off with a healthy perception.

• It can do wonders for your self-image. It's a good feeling to know that your boss and coworkers are depending on you to do a job that you know you can do. The rush of self-confidence may inspire you to run for mayor.

• It exposes you to new people—good and bad. You may

find yourself getting along great with people you'd have never picked as friends. Suddenly all your "rules" about who's cool and who isn't don't apply.

• Unlike much of what you learn in school, the things you

learn at work are put to use immediately. You don't learn things because you'll be graded on them; you learn them because you *need* to.

• You may do such a good job that your boss makes you vice president with access to the company jet and a condo on Maui.

IT'S THE LAW

Jack London (the guy who wrote *The Call of the Wild* and *The Sea Wolf* and lots of other great stories you really ought to read) had some tough jobs as a teenager around the turn of the century. At fifteen he worked ten hours a day in a cannery for one dollar a *day*. At eighteen he shoveled coal twelve hours a day, seven days a week, with one day off per month. His wage: thirty dollars per month.

Nowadays, to protect you from such horrible work, the government has strict laws about how many hours you can

I'M SORRY, SON, BECAUSE OF YOUR AGE WE CAN'T ALLOW YOU TO OPERATE SLICING MACHINES OR WORK ON SCAFFOLDING. WE ARE, HOWEVER, LOOKING FOR A FEW GOOD MEN.

work and the types of jobs you can do. The Fair Labor Standards Act is the federal law affecting anyone under eighteen. It says that you can't work during school hours or perform dangerous work—operate meat slicing machines, work on scaffolding, paint tigers' toenails, and so on.

If you're under sixteen, the above restrictions apply, plus a few more: you can't work more than three hours on a school day, work past seven at night, or put in more than eighteen hours during the week.

Each state has its own labor laws, which may be stricter than the federal law. Although the federal law doesn't require you to have a work permit, your state may. You can get the facts by talking to a school counselor or librarian or by calling the Employment or Labor Office listed under the State Government section of the phone book.

Your first work experiences are test drives. From these early jobs you'll learn what you like and dislike about certain kinds of work, and what you want to do in the future. During World War I a couple of fifteen-year-olds got an early job experience driving an ambulance. In the midst of their gruesome tasks they'd talk about the kind of work they wanted to do after the war. They dreamed about the kinds of businesses they'd start, how they'd manage them, how they'd treat employees. After the war these kids went off to do what they planned. Ray Kroc opened up a little chain of hamburger stands called Mc-Donalds; Walt Disney drew mouse cartoons and built Disneyland.[5] Your first job experiences can inspire you for even greater things.

Jobs Gone Bad

Teenage jobs can be great. But before you take one, you better look at the bad stuff:

• If you work too much during the school year, your education is going to suffer. Working late on school nights means you're going to sleep through your first two classes.

• If you spend all your time at school and work, your family may forget your name (clue: your Christmas gifts are marked, "To Occupant").

• You may lose valuable time for friends, sports, church, music, or some other important part of your life. (But if you have no friends, hobbies, or personality, a job will do you good.)

• Working after school each day will prevent you from watching "Leave It to Beaver."

And Now for the Ugly Part

Working long hours at an unchallenging job can do more than use up your time and energy: *it can make you cynical about work in general*. The job becomes a necessary evil that you're willing to tolerate until you can afford to quit it. Unfortunately, many of the jobs open to you are just that: don't think, just push these little buttons, take the money, give back the change shown on the computer screen, and say, "Have a nice day."

You know that companies are getting into computers and high technology in a big way. Fast-food outlets, stores, and equipment makers are busy trying to develop cash registers, scanners, broilers, fryers, and toasters that make jobs as easy—and as boring—as pushing buttons. They've managed to make some of these jobs almost mindless.

But if a job is too boring, employers have a tough time filling it. The average annual turnover among restaurant workers is 250 percent—that means the average worker keeps the job for less than five months. Many employees quit within thirty days of taking the job, so whatever training they received is wasted.[6] Some managers are so desperate they print job applications on placemats and hang permanent help wanted signs in the windows.

If an employer still can't find enough workers, she might start raising the wages. *Wall Street Journal* reporter Michele Manges theorizes that "a growing labor shortage, which would drive up pay, figures to draw more kids into those jobs—against their interests."[7]

Some of your friends are working in jobs that cost more in damage to their lives than the fattest paycheck can compensate for.

It's true. Some of your friends are working in jobs that pay well but cost far more in damage to their education, family, friendships, and self-image than the fattest paycheck can compensate for. So before you start hunting for a job, you've got some work to do:

• Consider how many hours you can afford to work without damaging your other priorities. (What's your bottom line?)

• Talk to friends who have jobs. Find out what they're learning—and the negative effects of their jobs on their lives.

• Look at who you are and how that will affect the kind of

job you might like: introvert, extrovert; organized, spontaneous; team player, lone ranger; early bird, night owl; frantic, methodical. A job that doesn't complement your personality can make you miserable.

• Talk to your parents. You can work for the next fifty years if you want to, but you can never buy back the time you'll lose with your family.

If you determine that a job isn't right for you at the moment, that's great! If you believe that a job would be a positive addition to your life, that's great, too. But the decision has to be yours.

WRITING A RESUME

Before you hunt for the job of your dreams, you should put together a resume, which is a summary of your most important work and educational *accomplishments*. At this point in your career you may be asking, "But what if I don't *have* any?" You do. And the reason you should write a resume before going out to look for a job is to show *yourself* how talented you are.

The first resume you should write is intended for your eyes only: don't plan on handing it out to potential employers. Its purpose is to convince you that you've had valuable experiences that will help you do any job better. Here's how to write a resume that works even if you've had little or no formal job experience.

1. List Your Job Experiences

List all volunteer or paid jobs you've had, no matter how small or insignificant they may seem. Under each job, identify the main responsibilities and accomplishments:

THE AVERAGE PLAYER'S SALARY FOR THE 1988 NEW YORK METS WAS $605,895.

• Newspaper Delivery Person. Delivered papers every day; solicited new subscribers; got few complaints; trained my replacement.

• Baby-sitter. Baby-sat for eight different families on regular basis: considered reliable by parents; well liked by kids.

• Concession Stand Salesclerk. Worked snack trailer at Little League a few times: sold food; operated cash register; cooked on the grill, learned how to set up the soda fountain.

• School Newspaper Reporter. Reporter for junior-high newspaper: wrote one article per month; interviewed principal, teachers, and students; learned editing, layout, paste-up, printing, and collating.

2. Identify Your Strengths

These jobs won't astound any potential employer. But they should convince you that you have strengths that make you very hirable:

• You know how to *work under pressure* (Little League concession stands are mob scenes after a game).

• You're *reliable* (the paper route and baby-sitting show you that).

HOW'S THE RESUME COMING?

I'M TRYING TO FIND AN IMPRESSIVE WAY TO SAY "I'VE SPENT MY LIFE SURFING."

• You're *trustworthy* (most parents won't trust the lives of their kids with losers).

• You know how to *work with a deadline* (being late is unforgivable for reporters and newspaper delivery persons).

• You're *teachable* (you learned new skills at the concession stand and the school paper).

• You *can teach others* (you trained your replacement on the newspaper route).

• You have *sales experience* (the concession stand and the newspaper route required you to sell things).

• You seem to *work well with adults* (you had to do that with all your jobs).

3. Measure Your Accomplishments

What's missing in your list is any measure of *how well* you did. So go back through it and try to quantify as many accomplishments as possible. As a newspaper delivery person you increased your route size 20 percent in three months by selling new subscriptions and got awarded on three occasions for zero-complaint months (don't mention that in another month you hit one cat and broke two windows).

In the baby-sitting department, you averaged five requests a week and baby-sat for one family over fifty times. At the concession stand you personally served up to fifty customers in one hour (and killed twelve cockroaches). And at the school newspaper you figured out a way to cut the printing time in half.

4. Put It All Together

You're beginning to look like Superworker. Rewrite your resume, organizing it by job strengths (e.g., trustworthy, teachable, sales experience). Under each of these headings, list the specific accomplishments using as many numbers as you can. After reading your finished resume a few times, you should be convinced that you have great strengths and useful job skills. And if you're convinced, you stand a good chance of convincing a potential employer.

If you're applying for a retail salesclerk position and the manager asks you if you've ever worked in a store before, you can reply, "No, but I've had some sales experience: I've worked at a baseball concession stand, handling as many as fifty customers in an hour; and I've sold newspaper subscriptions, increasing my paper route by 20 percent in three months. I know how to make customers smile, and I'm pretty good at figuring out what to do when they're not happy." That sounds more impressive than telling her that you sold hot dogs at a baseball game and got people to subscribe to the newspaper.

What's Next?

Lots of people say that you should type or print copies of your resume onto nice paper and give them out to potential employers. Others believe that if you don't have lots of job experience, there's no point in handing out a half-empty sheet of paper that proves it. Many employers go through stacks of applications when they're filling a position, so they don't have time to read a resume.

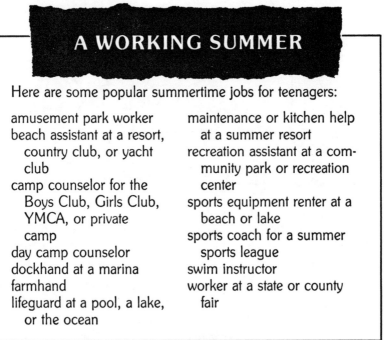

A WORKING SUMMER

Here are some popular summertime jobs for teenagers:

amusement park worker
beach assistant at a resort, country club, or yacht club
camp counselor for the Boys Club, Girls Club, YMCA, or private camp
day camp counselor
dockhand at a marina
farmhand
lifeguard at a pool, a lake, or the ocean
maintenance or kitchen help at a summer resort
recreation assistant at a community park or recreation center
sports equipment renter at a beach or lake
sports coach for a summer sports league
swim instructor
worker at a state or county fair

HELP WANTED—PART-TIME

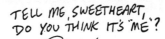

Here are some of the most popular part-time jobs available for teenage workers year-round:

assembler	nurse's aide, orderly
bagger	painter
cashier	receptionist
child-care worker	restaurant host, hostess
computer operator	retail sales clerk
construction worker	secretary, typist, data entry
food counter worker	clerk
framer	service station attendant
janitor, maid	shipping or warehouse
kitchen assistant	worker
mechanic	stock handler
	waitress, waiter

The job-finding ideas in the next chapter don't require a resume. If you think one is necessary or helpful, go ahead and put one together. But at this point in your career, the resume's essential task is to convince *you*.

3

NINE PROVEN (KIND OF) WAYS TO LAND A JOB

Armed with a clear idea of what you want from a job and the skills you can bring to it, you're ready to look for a job. These techniques will help you land one that fits in with your goals.

CONNECTIONS

If an employer has a choice, she'll hire someone she knows (or at least someone who knows someone she knows) before hiring a complete stranger. That means the best way to look for a job is not to search the want ads but to talk to your family and friends. Ask your parents if they have any friends who own businesses or can somehow help you find a job where they work. Ask your own friends about open positions at their jobs. If your friend is a good worker, his recommendation is worth a lot (and if he's a sloth, you may get *his* position).

TRADING PLACES

If you have a friend who is getting ready to quit a good job, you may be able to take her place. But the employer will do this only if your friend is a good worker; if she's not, he won't respect her opinion of other potential workers. You'll still have to sell yourself to the boss, but you've already got one foot in the door.

To make it even more attractive to the boss, have your friend offer to train you for free: work alongside her without pay during her last day; or have her work alongside you on your first day—and you pay for it out of your paycheck. You make it very easy for the employer because he doesn't have to go through all the trouble of searching, interviewing, hiring, and training.

And if you happen to look a lot like your friend, you may be able to do the switch without even telling the boss (but when payday comes, it may be tough to cash the check).

MEETING THE MANAGEMENT

About one-fourth of all employees find their jobs by applying directly with the employer.[8] Begin by making out a list of the ten places you'd most like to work. Do what you can to

learn the name of the manager at each business (the Chamber of Commerce can help you, or you can call the business and ask an employee for the name). Now go out and meet them.

Dress in clothes that you would wear on the job but a little bit nicer. At each site, your goal is to meet the manager. Walk in and ask for her by name: "Hi—I'd like to speak to Ms. Jacobsen, please" (this sounds much more important than asking for "the manager"). If she's not in, find out when she'll return, then come back later. Try not to tell the person that you're job hunting, since she'll either tell you there's nothing available or have you fill out an application—either way, you won't get to see the manager.

Whether you meet the manager on your first or thirteenth try, introduce yourself, then state your business: "Ms. Jacobsen, I'm Glen Richmond. I'd like to work for you." Okay, so it sounds bold and scary, but it's quick, honest, and to the point.

She'll probably do one of three things:

1. Interview you right there, and maybe even hire you.
2. Ask you to fill out an application—she'll call if she can use you.
3. Tell you there are no positions available.

If she chooses option 1, you've done well. If she chooses option 2, tell her you'd like to take the application with you and bring it back tomorrow. If she chooses option 3, you've still got a chance: "If you don't mind, I'd like to fill out an application anyway, in case a position opens up later." As with option 2, tell her you'd like to take the application home and return it tomorrow. (Taking the application home gives you an opportunity to fill it out neatly—and an excuse to come back the next day.)

When you leave, be sure to mark the name of the business

on the application. You're going to collect several of these from different places, and you want to return the right application to each one. Also write down the date and time of your visit and any other information you learned from meeting the manager. Now hit as many other sites on your list as you can.

At home, fill out each application you collected that day as neatly as you possibly can—you can even type it if you have bad printing. Now staple a good photo of yourself to the application (faces are easier to remember than names). The next day, go back and ask for the manager by name. Remind her of who you are: "Hi, Ms. Jacobsen. I'm Glen Richmond—I came in yesterday about a job. Here's my application." In these two brief meetings, you've told her everything she needs to know to hire you:

• You're reliable. (You said you would return the application the next day; you did what you said.)

• You're confident. (Many adults are surprised and pleased when a teenager introduces himself first.)

• You're eager. (Two visits, a typed application, a photo, you dressed nice—you're serious!)

• You're sharp. (You thought through your plan of attack.)

And she also knows your name and face. If she has a position available, she may just hire you on the spot. If not, your application will probably end up in a file with a bunch of others. But when it comes time to hire someone, whose application is she likely to remember?

Two weeks have passed and still no job offers. It's not over yet. Because most high-school and college students keep jobs for less than a year and often quit jobs with little or no warning, their employers are constantly looking for new workers on short notice. Sometimes they need a replacement immediately and don't have time to sort through a stack of applications to track down a replacement. If they get lots of applications, they might even throw out old ones every few weeks, figuring that those people have probably found other jobs by then.

That's why it's a good idea to drop in again to show your face to that potential boss. Give her your name and ask if there's any news on an opening. It's awkward to do this, so give yourself an excuse. Go in to buy something and say, "By the way. . . . " Or bring in your resume and ask, "I put this together and thought it might help someone sorting through applications. Could you attach it to mine?" (And if you're still in a bold mood: "Hi, Ms. Jacobsen—Glen Richmond again. I still want to work for you.")

If someone has just quit, you may be in the right place at the right time. If there isn't a job for you, she still knows your name and face better than any other applicant.

A word of warning: Don't overdo it. If you keep going back week after week, she'll remember you—as a pest.

NEW BUSINESS

Opening a new business is a major undertaking: getting permits, constructing or remodeling the space, buying and installing equipment and furniture, stocking inventory, and hiring and training new employees. You may be able to help out a new business owner or manager with this last step.

If you see a new store or business being put into a mall or shopping center, go to the building's management office and get the name and phone number of the owner or manager. Call and tell her you'd like to work in the new store, and you're available now. If she agrees to hire you, you're one less person she needs to worry about the week before the grand opening when things get really crazy and time is short. You may be able to start early by helping set up the store.

Helping launch a business is tough work, but you'll learn more from the experience than you can from almost any other kind of job.

SOURCE SEARCH

In addition to the newspaper want ads, several organizations list job opportunities:

• The Chamber of Commerce may list summer job opportunities.

• The Labor Department's U.S. Employment Service has offices in many cities throughout the country that list jobs. You can call the local office by finding the number in the government section of the phone book.

• Your state, county, or city may also have an employment office.

• If you haven't already done so, check the job listings in your school's career center.

• Many YMCAs, churches, and other community organizations sponsor job boards listing part-time and summer jobs open to teens. Get out the phone book and call as many of these organizations as you can locate. Even if they don't have a job board, they may want to fill a job for which you qualify.

COLLEGE JOBS

Employers who can afford to pay higher wages for part-time help will seek college students, who they hope will be more reliable and mature than high schoolers. To get them, they often advertise on job boards at the local college. Most colleges have a bulletin board or office that posts positions of interest to students.

Go to the college and get the information on any openings you're interested in. Visit each potential employer. Introduce yourself in the manner described under "Meeting the Management," but be sure to mention that you read about the job at the college. (You don't need to tell him that you're not a college student unless he asks.) If you follow the same method, you should be able to prove you're as reliable and mature as any college student he's likely to hire.

DIRECT MAIL

If you're looking for a position in a professional office (working for a physician, attorney, architect, broker, accountant), popping in on the office manager may not be a good idea. Instead, send a letter.

Actually, to get the job you want you may need to send dozens of letters. Maybe you're really interested in architecture, and you'd like to get a job as an office assistant at an architectural firm. Use the phone book to get a list of architects in your area (the Chamber of Commerce should also be able to help you). Draft a letter that you can send to each name on your list. The easiest way to do this, of course, is with a personal computer: write one letter in the word processing program, load all the names and addresses in a merge file, and let the computer print a personalized letter to each prospective employer. Or if you don't have access to a computer, use a typewriter. Print the letters on the nicest white stationery you can find. (Check an office supply store.)

Your letter should be short, enthusiastic, and intriguing enough to make the recipient want to call you.

You may have to send out dozens of these letters to get just one response, so mail as many as you can. If you get any response at all, it will come the day the letter is delivered, or within two or three days after that. During those critical days, make sure you're at home answering the phone every time it rings. If you can't be there, make sure that whoever is there takes a clear message and tells the caller that you'll return the call as soon as you can.

Don't bother to send a resume with this kind of letter. The letter itself should tell the person just enough to get him interested. If you send a resume, he may give your letter to his secretary or office manager without even reading it. Then that person will put it in a file with all the other resumes and applications, which defeats the whole purpose of the letter: to stand out as someone worth calling.

If you hear nothing after a week, you may want to follow up with a few of the most desirable firms by making a phone call to the letter's recipient: "Hi, Mr. Martinez . . . did you get my letter?"

234 Las Colinas Ave.
Coronado, CA 92017
February 21, 1991

Mr. Michael Martinez
Martinez & Hunt
1369 Center Drive
San Diego, CA 92012

Dear Mr. Martinez:

I work hard, learn quickly, and believe in doing the job right.

I'm writing you this letter in case you're looking for a part-time office assistant. Here's a little more about me:

- junior at Eastside High School with a 3.40 GPA
- three years of drafting courses
- type 40 wpm
- can operate a blueprint machine, facsimile, personal computer
- excellent driving record
- planning to pursue a career in architecture

If you're interested in learning more about me and how I might be an asset to your office, please call me at 458-1243. I would be happy to meet with you.

Sincerely,

Anna Weese

WORK FOR FREE

Some jobs are worth going through drastic measures to get. Lots of students are willing to take a nonpaid internship

just to get a foot in the door. If you're a hard worker and a paid position eventually opens up, you're in the ideal place for it.

To get an internship on your own, introduce yourself to the manager, owner, or professional you want to work for. Tell her you are eager to work for no pay in exchange for the training and experience. Also make it clear that you would like to be

considered for a paid position if you prove your worth and a job becomes available, but you understand that there's no guarantee.

If the employer senses that you're sincerely interested in the opportunity and not a vulture hovering around until someone quits, dies, or gets fired, she may take you on.

CREATE A POSITION

Sometimes you can convince an employer to hire you by creating a new product or service for his business. Let's say you're interested in graphic art and screen printing. Approach the officers of a few clubs at your school to see if they would like custom T-shirts printed for their members (you can also do this with the sports teams). If there's enough interest, go to a screen-printing shop with a proposition: you'll line up new customers and orders from your campus if the manager will hire you.

Like most business deals, there are many ways to arrange this:

1. You can be paid a commission on each order from these new customers.

2. You can become an hourly worker and "give" the shop the new business in exchange for the work experience.

3. If you have the experience but not the printing setup, you may be able to "rent" the shop and equipment during off-hours on a per-job basis.

Of course, you don't want to divulge the names of the potential customers until you have a deal in writing; this will help prevent the shop from taking your idea without you.

Other jobs you might be able to create: selling corsages and boutonnieres for a florist; teaching art courses at a day-care center; providing a home delivery service for a pharmacy, florist, restaurant, or market.

4

DON'T SPIT.
AND OTHER HOT TIPS FOR
A WINNING INTERVIEW

Advertising agencies know that if their ad doesn't grab the reader in that first second or so, she won't bother to read any further. An ad that fails in the first second is a failure—regardless of how good the rest of the ad is or the quality of the product it sells. Now imagine that you and everyone else looking for a job are just advertisements in a magazine. The employer is flipping through the magazine very fast, deciding every moment whether to read an ad or turn the page.

Fortunately, if you've managed to meet the boss face-to-face, you have more than a few seconds to make your impression. You have an entire minute! In that first minute of an introduction or an interview, your potential employer is going to make some important decisions about you. You need to make every second count.

DRESS

Wear what you'd wear on the job if you were hired. If you're unsure, it's better to overdress than underdress. But make sure you feel comfortable—if it makes you *feel* strange, you'll *look* strange.

GROOMING

Some tips to prepare yourself:

• Fix your hair so it stays out of your eyes. Compulsive adults will be thinking of how to shove it out of the way.

• Don't wear a lot of cologne, perfume, or aftershave. (Hint: If they smell you before they see you, it's too much.)

• Try not to smell like tobacco, gasoline, or a wet dog.

• Get the cat hair off your sweater.

• Remove the Milk Duds debris from your teeth.

• Avoid makeup that looks like it was applied while you were riding on a motorcycle. This is especially important for girls.

• Use a breath mint.

BODY LANGUAGE

You can make clear and positive statements about yourself without opening your mouth:

• Offer to shake hands when you meet. Age and sex don't matter. Give a firm, friendly grip, look into the person's eyes and smile. (Translation: *Meeting you is important to me.*)

• Look directly at the person's face when you speak. (*I believe in what I'm saying.*)

• Do the same when you're listening to people. (*I care about what you're saying.*)

• Don't put paper clips in your nose. (*I can be trusted with office supplies.*)

POSTURE

You can tell a lot about a person by the way he walks, stands, and sits. There are some examples of good and bad posture on the following page.

MINIMUM WAGE IN 1950: 75 CENTS PER HOUR.

GOOD   BAD

GOOD   BAD

GOOD   BAD

WHAT TO SAY

Your ability to communicate is being evaluated. Speak in your normal voice and follow these tips:

• When meeting someone, state your name clearly. If the person has forgotten your name, you save her the embarrassment of having to ask.

• Address an adult by his or her last name (e.g., Mr. Rogers, Ms. Piggy) until you're given permission to use the first name. Use the name frequently—people like to hear their names.

• Don't use swear words unless you have a note from your mom.

HOW TO MAKE A LOUSY FIRST IMPRESSION

• Ask, "How long do you think it would take me to get your job?"

• Tell her all the times you're not available.

• Bring along a friend and insist that hiring you is a package deal.

• Bring your grandmother with you.

• Trim your toenails.

• Ask if you can smoke a cigar while you're meeting.

• Eat an anchovy sandwich immediately beforehand.

• Tell her the family picture on her desk reminds you of a trip you took to the zoo.

• Chew gum: blow bubbles, stick it on your nose, then under the chair.

• Point and say, "Nice tie!" Then laugh very loud.

MINIMUM WAGE IN 1960: $1.00 PER HOUR.

HOW TO LOOK OLDER

If you look young for your age, here are some things you can do to age yourself:

- Dress conservatively.
- Walk slower and stand taller than usual.
- Pause before speaking.
- Don't talk with your hands.
- Wear a fake moustache (most effective with guys).
- Remove the Chiquita Bananas sticker from your fore-head.
- Don't come in holding your mom's hand.

JOB INTERVIEWS

Making the right impression is important anytime you meet a potential employer. But when you're sitting down for a full job interview, you're after more than a good first impression: you're going for a great lasting impression. Here's how.

GEE, I HOPE I'M NOT GOING TO HAVE TO HANDLE DETAILS. I'VE NEVER BEEN TOO GOOD WITH DETAILS.

Before the Interview

Find out as much as you can about the business. If it's a big company, details about it probably appear in one of the corporate directories at the library—ask the librarian where to look. You can also call friends who've worked there. The more you know, the more intelligent you'll sound during your interview. It will also be obvious to your prospective employer that you care enough to do some homework. Make a list of your questions about the job responsibilities and expectations and about the company in general. The answers will help you decide if the job is right for you.

Write out questions you're likely to be asked. Have a friend or family member interview you using these questions so you can get comfortable talking about yourself. This will also teach you how to answer questions succinctly (short and to the point).

YEAH, WELL, I DID HAVE A JOB LAST SUMMER, BUT, LIKE, THE BOSS WAS ALWAYS SAYING THAT I, UH, DIDN'T PAY ATTENTION. SO...UM...

WELL... AND THEN I THOUGHT

Here are some questions you may be asked:

What can you tell me about yourself? Make it short and sweet: your school, grade, family, interests.

What subjects do you enjoy? Why? Be honest; show enthusiasm over things you like.

Sports? Hobbies? Other interests? Again, show enthusiasm and a sense of dedication for the things you care about.

Do you drive? Own a car? What he's really asking: "Can you be counted upon to get here on time?" and "Can you run errands that require driving?" If you don't have a car, assure him that you have a reliable means of getting to work.

What are your strengths? What he wants to hear: "I work hard, I learn fast, and I'm reliable." If it's true, say it.

What are your weaknesses? "Acceptable" weaknesses involve having too much of a good thing: perfectionist, too task-oriented, overly self-critical.

What are your future plans? Anything ambitious sounds better than "I don't really know."

What days and hours can you work? Have a copy of your schedule; be honest about nonnegotiables—school, study, church, family time.

Why do you want to work here? Good place to work, challenging, nice coworkers, good reputation, quality product—whatever is true.

At the Interview

Show up a few minutes early; make sure your hair, face, teeth, and elbows are in order. Bring a notepad and your questions with you. Also bring along an extra pen: a mean-spirited federal statute (hustled through Congress by the pencil lobby) requires pen manufacturers to design their pens in such a way that a certain percentage will run out of ink in the middle of a job interview.

While you're waiting for the interview, casually look around

MINIMUM WAGE IN 1970: $1.60 PER HOUR.

SO! WHAT'S THE SQUARE ROOT OF 246 TIMES 7³ AND HOW DOES THIS RELATE TO THE AGRICULTURAL RELATIONSHIP BETWEEN IDAHO AND OUR COMPANY?

and see if any of the workers are watching you. If one employee seems to be staring, she's probably afraid she is about to be fired and you're going to get her job. *What do you have that she doesn't? Why are you so special?*

You wish you could tell her not to worry. You're not interviewing for her job. But how do you know that? Maybe you are. No, the manager said it was for a new position. But of course, that's what he has to say. He doesn't want her to know she's history until he's hired a replacement. What if you are her replacement? No wonder she's sneering. Maybe she hates you for it.

Or maybe she hates you for another reason. Maybe she's

thinking you're not here for a job at all. The "interview" story is just your cover—you're an undercover detective hired to prove that she was the one who embezzled the $5,000. Is she starting to sweat? Does she rub her wrists, wondering what the handcuffs will feel like?

Oh, no, she's reaching into the desk drawer for something. What is it? Scissors! She's coming for you! You plead with her: "Look, I don't know anything . . . I'm just here for a job—not your job, someone else's—don't hurt me!"

"I'm not going to hurt you. You have a loose thread on your shirt. Sit still and I'll get it for you."

If you survive your imagination and make it into the interview, here's what's next. Your goal: to convey as many of your positive traits before bringing up any negatives. In other words, you're a salesperson, and the product you're selling is you.

When you feel it's appropriate, start asking your questions. The kinds of questions you ask will tell the manager a lot about you: you're smart, not afraid to ask questions, and interested in the job. Take a few notes on the answers. People speak more carefully when their answers are being written down. But don't get carried away—there's no quiz afterward, so there's no need to appear like a crazed student.

Try not to bring up hours, vacation, pay, and benefits until the end. If you've sold yourself well in the first part of the interview, he'll be much more flexible about these things. (The stereo salesman sells you on the sound and features until you're in love, then he hits you with the price: it's hard to say no to something you love.)

At the end of the interview, find out when you could expect to receive an offer if the interviewer decides to make one. Then thank him with a handshake.

MINIMUM WAGE IN 1980: $3.10 PER HOUR.

Other interview helps:

• Convey what makes you unique. You want to be remembered.

• Show interest in the job, not the money.
• Remember that employers don't expect teenagers to be experts when they hire them. They're looking for enthusiasm, eagerness to learn, a cooperative spirit, and reliability. If you can get that message across in your interview, you've done the best you can.
• Every interview is a priceless lesson: take notes, learn from your mistakes, look back and laugh, and get better.
• Never start a water balloon fight during a job interview (but if someone else throws the first balloon, go for the kill).

After the Interview

Send a thank-you letter to the person who interviewed you. If there was more than one interviewer, write the note to the one who has the power to hire you. Mail the letter that day so the person doesn't have an opportunity to forget you.

Now continue your job search: meet managers and line up interviews. Keep working at it. Your goal is to have at least two or three offers to choose from.

5

HANDLING JOB OFFERS
AND REJECTIONS

A job interview is kind of like a pass-fail exam. If you pass, they call you back. If you fail, you don't hear from them.

When you get a job offer, generally by phone, thank the person sincerely. Write down the details: starting date, wage, hours, and so on. Tell the employer that you'd like to accept but you need a day to discuss it with your family. Now talk it over with your parents and some close friends. Compare the job offer to your original goals. Sometimes in the excitement of landing a job you can lose sight of your own best interests.

If you applied anywhere else for a position that you'd rather have than the one being offered, call that employer. Explain that you got another job offer but would rather work for him. If he can give you a good offer, you'll take his instead. If he says no, you can accept the first offer. If he offers you a better job, you're set. You have a job either way, and you can be confident that you got the best deal available.

When No One Calls

Unless the employer has specifically told you not to, it's appropriate to call back in a week to find out if there's any news. If the position is still open, you have one more opportunity to be heard from; if it's filled, you can move on. If you've done this right, you have several other businesses considering you, so you can continue to pursue them.

Rejections

No matter how wonderful you are, you're going to be rejected many times in your life. Maybe not the first time you look for a job, but sooner or later, you'll get turned down. There are a hundred reasons why you'll get rejected for a job, and most are beyond your control. A few:

• The employer got a tax bill and realized she couldn't afford to hire anyone.

- She once had a terrible worker with the same name as yours, so she subconsciously ruled you out.
- An old employee wanted her job back; giving it to her was easier than training someone new.
- The manager was forced to hire the owner's nephew, Winthrop.
- Your application got thrown out by mistake.
- Something in your manner reminds her of her uncle Hubert, whom she can't stand.
- She called your number twice: the first time there was no answer; the second time it was busy, so she went to the next applicant.
- Your personality rubbed her the wrong way.

IN 1990, NEW ZEALAND STOPPED THE USE OF THEIR ONE-CENT AND TWO-CENT COINS.

I'M SORRY, I'M JUST NOT SURE YOU'D BE QUITE RIGHT FOR THE JOB.

• You looked too smart to be satisfied with such a low-paying job for very long.

Lots of times the employer can tell you wouldn't be right for the job. She understands her business, and she knows you'd be miserable in a few months. These kinds of rejections aren't fun, but in the end you're happier because of them.

Bad Sale

Sometimes you don't get the job because you conveyed the wrong message. Here are some of the reasons employers give for not hiring student workers:[9]

- poor personal appearance
- overbearing, know-it-all
- inability to express self clearly, poor diction and grammar
- lack of interest, enthusiasm
- interested only in paycheck
- wants too much too soon
- makes excuses, is evasive
- tactless
- discourteous
- lack of vitality
- little sense of humor
- lazy

If you come off in one or more of these ways during an interview, you'll need to work on fixing the problem. Every interview is a lesson in selling yourself—something you'll have to do for the rest of your life. Learn from your mistakes and do a better job next time.

No one likes rejection. No one is immune to its pain. It cuts some people deeper than others, and lots of folks are experts at smiling on the outside while they're dying on the inside. When you've been rejected, it's okay to "let it get you down" (despite what everyone is so quick to advise).

Just know that the quickest way to stop feeling bad is to go back out there, give a winning interview, and land an exciting job.

6

HOW TO KEEP A JOB YOU LIKE

I've hated every job I've ever had . . . for the first month. The first weeks of a new job are miserable. I forget everyone's name, and when I remember, I get them mixed up: "My name's not Ralph—it's Rebecca!" I become so self-conscious that I forget not only everything I've just been taught but also everything I've ever been taught: multiplication tables, how to tie shoes, and the whole concept of opening the door before trying to leave the room.

After the first month I become normal again (relatively speaking) and start to enjoy the job.

Most employers understand that your first few weeks may be rough, and they generally cut you some slack. But there comes a time when you had better do your job right. If you want to keep it, you'll have to deliver.

LEARN EVERYTHING YOU CAN

Most teenagers think the reason they're working is for the money. But if you're not learning everything you can on that job, you're making a lousy investment of your time and energy.

Training new workers is an expensive and tiring task for managers—sometimes they'd rather keep a mediocre employee than go through the hassle of hiring and training a new one. Knowledge is job insurance. The more you know, the harder you are to replace.

On-the-job learning pays dividends in other ways:

- You won't get bored when things are slow.
- You can teach others what you know. If you're good at it, you're in the best position to get a promotion.
- What you learn may help in future jobs; it can also help you successfully launch your own business.

Paid to Learn

The thing that prevents most people from learning is their stubbornness. For example, every time the photocopier jams, Sandy has to ask someone else to fix it for her. Her excuse: "I'm not mechanically inclined." She can drive a car, use a typewriter, and program a VCR, but she refuses to learn the five simple steps to clearing the copier's paper path.

There's nothing wrong with not being mechanically inclined. Just don't apply for jobs repairing jet engines or designing oil refineries.

Knowledge is job insurance: the more you know, the harder you are to replace.

When I was nineteen, I worked in a small hospital. One day both the cook and his assistant went home sick. In two hours there would be 120 people waiting for their dinners, so the supervisor began a frantic search among the staff to find a cook. I volunteered. (I'd cooked scrambled eggs before, and I knew how to heat up soup.)

I read the menu plan, switched around some things that were too difficult to prepare, and started cooking. I made a few calls to friends for answers to important questions (how to put out a grease fire, how to make the chef's hat poof out at the top). I served the meal on time, everyone was happy, and the supervisor asked me to do the next meal, too. A few years later I handled the meals for my own youth camps—something I had the confidence to do because of that experience. Now when I cook, people say it tastes like hospital food. I don't know why.

"IF AT FIRST YOU DON'T SUCCEED YOU'RE RUNNING ABOUT AVERAGE."—M. H. Alderson

Make a list of tasks being performed where you work, from loading receipt paper into the cash register to reordering merchandise from a supplier. If your usual responsibilities are covered, pick something off the list and ask someone to teach you. Think of it this way: unlike school, you're actually getting paid to learn. Grasp every opportunity to do so.

DO WHAT'S RIGHT

Your job is one of the toughest proving grounds for your integrity. Behavior that's clearly wrong at home or among friends is standard conduct at the workplace. Many people who disapprove of lying, cheating, and stealing have no problem calling in sick when they aren't, stretching the hours on their time card, or taking home supposedly free merchandise. If you want to keep your job, behave according to what you know is right, not according to the code of ethics you see other workers following.

Behave according to what you know is right, not according to the code of ethics you see others following.

That's not an easy thing to do. In lots of jobs, it seems impossible NOT to cheat. The problem with cheating is that it's so habit-forming—it's a thrill to rearrange reality to suit your tastes. And the thrill that you're getting something for nothing is delightful because you can remember so many times when you got nothing after working your backside off. But if you cheat enough, trying to cope with life "as is"—without rearranging the facts—becomes a real chore. And it doesn't take long. Cheating is a strong drug.

Cheating and Being Cheated

It's true: cheaters do prosper. But amazingly enough, so can honest people. Maybe not as fast, or as great, but honest people attain their goals without sacrificing their character. Sometime in their lives most people stop being consumed by where they're going and pay more attention to how they're getting there.

Work would be so much more fun if everyone played by those rules. But you're stuck working with and for people who lie, cheat, and steal to get ahead. Sooner or later someone will nail you: cheat you out of a commission, deny you a "guaranteed" raise, take the credit for your idea.

SALARY MEANS SALT MONEY, FROM THE DAYS WHEN ROMAN SOLDIERS WERE GIVEN MONEY TO BUY SALT TO PRESERVE THEIR FOOD.

The most dangerous cheaters are bosses. Someday you'll have a boss who will promise one thing and do another, then deny he ever made the promise. He'll manipulate to get more work out of you for the same pay or even get you to work "off the clock"—for free. He'll go to his boss with your accomplishments and claim them as his own, then give you the "credit" for his mistakes. He's a slime.

Slimes are a fact of life. There are two things you can do: protect yourself from them as best you can, and never, never become like them.

Slime Protection

When you buy an item, you keep the receipt; if something is wrong with the merchandise, you can prove where you bought it and how much you paid. Businesspeople sign contracts to ensure that they'll get what was promised. Teachers give you tests to see written evidence that you know the material. Documents help us communicate better and protect ourselves from unscrupulous people.

If you have any reason to question your boss's memory or business integrity, get wage and raise agreements in writing. As carefully and politely as possible, ask him to write the terms on a piece of paper for you. If he's likely to be hurt by your apparent mistrust, tell him your parents are protective and insist on seeing these things. (Don't lie about it: ask your parents to insist—few things enrage them more than seeing one of their children being cheated by an adult.*)

Without a written agreement, it's easy for a boss to cheat you. Let's say he comes to you in October with news about your overdue raise: "You deserve a fifty-cent raise, but I can't afford to do it until after the new year begins. If you'll hang in there and work at your present rate, I'll give you a seventy-five-cent raise in January."

You agree, but the Christmas rush doesn't ring up as much in sales as expected, so your boss "forgets" the deal. It's February and you remind him. He remembers saying, "If the Christmas rush is strong, I'll give you a raise." But because that didn't happen, he says he's willing to give you a sixty-cent raise, effective starting in March.

You just lost $120 (75¢ per hour × 80 hours per month × January and February)—even more if you count the 50¢ raise you never got months ago.

If you had asked for a note describing the arrangement back in October, this wouldn't have happened. Now consider another possibility. What if he was right, and you heard him

---

*Remember in the third grade when the umpire called you "out"—and your mom almost strangled him?

wrong? The note would have protected him from your mistake. With a written agreement, you're both protected.

You can protect some of your ideas the same way. If you come up with a good one, write it down on a sheet of paper and date the note. Make a copy of it for yourself, and give your boss the original.

There's no way to make yourself completely immune to the bites of dirty-dealing people. But you can protect yourself from some of the ill effects.

GIVE THE BOSS A BREAK

Most bosses are easy to please. Some employers have put up with so many irresponsible workers that one who simply shows up on time makes employee of the month. I've noted five traits at the top of a boss's description of the ideal employee.

Punctuality. Showing up late, leaving early, and failing to come at all are among an employer's biggest headaches with employees. When you're supposed to be there but aren't, either work isn't being done, or people more responsible than

you are taking up the slack. If you think changing your habits to get to work on time is tough now, wait until you're twenty-five or thirty and that habit is as much a part of you as your name. It's now or never.

Show up five minutes early every day. Every week that you have a perfect attendance record, treat yourself to a frozen yogurt or some other reward. Don't call in sick unless you're sick—nobody likes being lied to. If you've agreed to work that day, do it. If you'd like a day off, plan ahead: get someone to work for you, or shoot straight with your boss.

Cooperation. Almost every job is a team effort. It doesn't matter how well you work if you can't get along with others. Sometimes being a boss is like being the referee of a profes-

sional wrestling match: employees gossiping, backbiting, fighting, and occasionally dragging the boss into the skirmish. Play fair, do your best to get along with others, and follow directions. You'll be a hit!

Initiative. Just do it. Nike's famous slogan applies in your job. Until you do, you're just a machine: you're told to do something and you do it. Initiative is a human trait. You decide for yourself that you'll do something, so you do it. Make a list of the things your boss tells you to do. The next day, do them all before he has a chance to remind you.

Enthusiasm. On the job there's one thing worse than being unhappy: being the boss of someone who's unhappy. If you have any reason to be excited about your job, let it show. Enthusiasm is contagious; the goal is to contaminate everyone you can.

Honesty. Lying about the number of hours you worked, giving out freebies to your friends, helping yourself to merchandise without permission—it seems like everyone does these things. But not quite everyone. There actually are a few honest people left, and they refuse to lie, cheat, or steal. Be one.

HAVE FUN

It's okay to have fun at work. There are very few jobs where it's inappropriate to laugh, smile, or joke with customers and coworkers. If you're getting your job done, not destroying things, or not offending people, you're probably making your workplace more pleasant for workers and customers. With a little creativity, you can turn even a boring job into a fun experience.

BAD PROMOTIONS

One of the most rewarding work experiences is getting a promotion. Yet a few promotions that sound great turn out to be bad deals. Before accepting any promotion or job change, you ought to take a day to think it over. Here are some popular "promotions" that can hurt you:

From hourly wages to a salary. If you work lots of overtime, an employer may want to "promote" you to a salary to avoid paying time-and-a-half wages. You end up working the same number of hours but getting a smaller paycheck. Of course, this isn't always true—just take a moment to add up the numbers before you say yes.

Trial promotion. She gives you a temporary promotion to fill a vacancy but doesn't pay any extra. Instead, she promises you that you'll get the position and raise if you prove yourself during the "trial" period. She can now take her time to find the right person for the job; until then she's getting the job done for less money than she was paying before. If she gives you the permanent position and the raise, you may feel cheated that you didn't get paid that amount for all the time you did the job. If she hires someone else, you'll feel like you failed and got nothing for all your effort; and going back to your old position may be difficult.

New title, more work, same pay. She knows that the prestige of an important-sounding title and the thrill of a promotion will distract you from the fact that you're doing more work for the same money. You're afraid of seeming ungrateful or greedy by bringing up the subject of a raise, so you keep quiet.

Counting the Cost

When you're faced with a promotion, remember to weigh the pay and education you'll receive against the time you'll be giving your employer. Is he paying you enough for the time you spend away from family, friends, and study? Because he pays you hourly doesn't mean he's buying only your time. Is he paying you fairly for your skills? Is he paying you fairly for the responsibilities you'll assume?

7

HOW TO QUIT AND HOW TO GET FIRED

A job can be a great thing to have, but it can also be the last thing you need right now. Every semester you need to ask yourself the same question: Do the pressures and conflicts, as well as less time for studying, friendships, family, and other activities, outweigh the benefits of the money and experience? If so, it's time to quit.

There are other reasons to quit:

• You have an unresolvable conflict with a boss or co-worker.

• You're forced to work under unsafe conditions.

• You're moving to Tasmania.

• You or your employer is doing something you believe to be immoral or illegal.

• Coworkers are having a negative influence on your behavior or attitude.

• You're being sexually or physically harassed.

• You've found a job that suits your needs better.

• You keep having dreams about knocking off your boss.

Whatever your reasons, carefully write out all of the positive and negative aspects of the job. The next time you look for a job, review the list. That way you can avoid getting yourself into a similar situation.

GOING OUT IN STYLE

The next step is to tell your boss. If you're a bad worker, she may leap for joy and be so excited about being saved from the trouble of firing you that she won't even bother to ask for a reason.

YOU'RE QUITTING! YOU'RE QUITTING!

But if you've been a good worker, she's likely to demand a reason for your decision to quit. Know your honest reason before she asks or else you might get talked into staying, or you might start an argument, or you might even make an enemy. If it's the money, tell her—but be ready for the possibility that she'll offer you more.

If you've found a better job, tell her. If the reason why the new job is better is beyond her control (e.g., closer to home, related to your career interests, better hours, it pays $100 an hour), let her know so she won't feel personally responsible. If your reason for quitting is to have more time for family, friends, school, church, or lawn bowling, say it.

If she's the reason why you're leaving, it's usually best not to say that in so many words (unless you have a very good relationship and think that she would want to know). Tell her the other job will work better for you—and if she digs for deeper reasons, mention one or two of your secondary reasons for making the switch. Arguing about her weaknesses isn't your responsibility. If you get into this kind of argument, she might (a) punch you in the nose, (b) give you a bad recommendation, (c) take it out on your friends who still work there, or (d) all of the above.

When you state your intention to leave, let her have two weeks' notice to give her time to find a replacement. However, she may find it more convenient for you to go immediately— someone may have been in that day looking for a job. She also may keep you on until you start acting like you're leaving, working with an "I don't care anymore" attitude. If you want to work for the next two weeks—and get a good recommendation for your next job—you're going to have to work at it.

HOW TO GET FIRED

If you're shy about saying, "I quit," you can usually irritate an employer to the point that he tells you to leave. Here are some behaviors to help him make up his mind.

Power Tardies

Determine how many minutes late you should arrive by raising the number ten to a power equal to the number of days worked until you're fired:

Day 1: 10^1 = 10 minutes late
Day 2: 10^2 = 100 minutes late
Day 3: 10^3 = 1,000 minutes late (16 hours, 40 minutes)
Day 4: 10^4 = 10,000 minutes late (1 week)
Day 5: 10^5 = 100,000 minutes late (69 1/2 days)
Day 6: 10^6 = 1,000,000 minutes late (2 years)

Salad Bar Brawl

If you work in a restaurant with a salad bar, post yourself at one end of the bar, armed with a long pair of tongs (you're welcome). Watch customers to make sure they don't drop broccoli bits in the potato salad or spill ranch dressing in the low-cal French. If someone makes a mess, use the tongs to tweak him on the nose. If he still refuses to clean it up, dump his plate out and send him to the end of the line. Should a customer complain to your boss, start a food fight: open fire with croutons and three-bean salad; cut down the enemy's visibility with clouds of cottage cheese and crumbled-up hard-boiled eggs. Now make for the door, pouring oil and vinegar dressing across the entrance to prevent a counterattack.

SIR, I FOUND THIS MAN AT THE SALAD BAR DROPPING BACON BITS ONTO THE COUNTER THAT I JUST CLEANED!

Boss for a Day

Quietly lock your boss in the supply closet when no one is looking. Tell the other employees that he had to leave the country for an indefinite period—something about an escaped convict—and he's appointed you as the new boss. If anyone objects, fire her. Give raises to the people you like, and schedule the next employee meeting for tomorrow . . . in the Bahamas. Call the travel agent, book the flights, and use the petty cash to buy flowered shirts for everyone.

8

THINGS YOU CAN DO TO PEOPLE WHEN YOU'RE THE BOSS

So they made you a boss. New title, new responsibilities, new money (if you're fortunate). And the power to tell other people what to do (get my coffee, shine my shoes, do ten push-ups). Actually, you probably know that being a leader involves mostly what you do *for* other people—not *to* them. Here are some tips to help you be a boss without being bossy.

PLAY FAIR

Each of us has a built-in justice meter; it instantly tells us if we're being treated unfairly. If we sense any kind of injustice against us—favoritism, backstabbing, discrimination—a red light in the brain starts blinking (really) and we cry out, "That's not fair!"

If you're an unfair boss, your workers may not tell you. They fear that you'll attribute their complaint to jealousy on their part rather than favoritism on yours. Instead, they'll hold grudges, gossip, and complain to one another, and they'll fight with one another to attain your favor. Or they may just slash your tires.

If you're a fair boss, workers will stop worrying about "getting what they deserve" and concentrate on doing a good job. Okay, so you'll still have a few problems from workers with tweaked justice meters. You can't have everything.

A primary job as a boss is upholding justice.

• *Praises*. If someone does something right, praise her. But if two people are worthy of praise and you neglect one of them, you're being unfair—and the neglected person knows it. It's like when your mother praises your little brother but fails to see much good in you. After a while, you just give up trying to please your mom and turn your attention toward stuffing your brother in the clothes dryer.

• *Hours and positions*. Some people are professional manipulators, always getting the hours they want without alarming you to what they're doing. When you make decisions on jobs and hours, do so with a list of all employees in front of you. You'll be able to spot whether someone always seems to get a much better deal than the others.

• *Looks and dress*. It's true—the good-looking people of the world get the most attention. It's not a romantic thing, just human nature. They're more pleasant to be around so you give them more of your time. If you want to be a fair boss, pay close attention to your attentions. Affirm people for who they are; encourage them in what they do. Forget what they look like.

YOU'RE THE BUTLER, YOU'RE THE MAID

Most firms' organizational charts put the head honcho at the top. Beneath her are the vice honchos, the rest of the salaried honchos, then the hourly workers at the very bottom.

"BY WORKING FAITHFULLY EIGHT HOURS A DAY, YOU MAY EVENTUALLY GET TO BE A BOSS AND WORK TWELVE HOURS A DAY."—Robert Frost

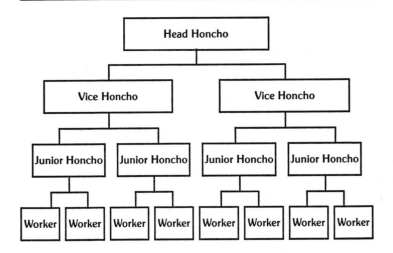

A few companies flip the chart. They put the big cheeses at the bottom, the medium cheeses above them, and so on, with the hourly workers near the top. The customers go at the very top of the chart.

This kind of an organizational chart makes a big statement: the customer comes first. The workers are the next level down, and their job is to serve the customers. The bosses are arranged beneath them, with the task of serving the workers. This goes on all the way down the chart. That makes you the *servant* of the people you supervise. Your job is to do what it takes to make them happy, excited, and effective in their jobs.

A good servant anticipates the needs of his masters, taking care of them before being asked. Train people so they can do their jobs better. Treat them fairly so they can worry about customers instead of discrimination. Praise them so they can feel good about themselves and their work. And every once in a while, serve them tea and biscuits on a silver tray.

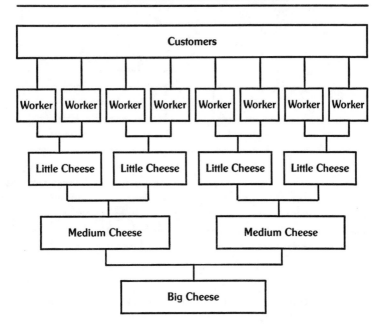

BE BIG

As a kid, if I found a scary bug in my room that I was too frightened to kill, my dad would always come in and do the job. He never cleaned my room or made the bed, but he could be counted upon to squash the scary bugs. Now I have my own place, and I can't call him up for an execution anymore (okay, I tried once, but the bug crawled away before his plane landed). It's my job now. It comes with the territory.

When you're a boss, you've got to be big sometimes. People are looking for a leader, and you're it. That means squashing bugs, stopping fights, handing out praise, making impossible decisions, and fixing other people's mistakes. That's one of the reasons why you get paid more. Look around you and try to find some tasks that won't get done unless you're big enough to do them.

I'M THE BOSS.

AND THIS BUG-SQUASHER PROVES IT !

SAY YOU'RE WRONG

There are two voices in your brain. The first says, "If I admit my mistakes, I'll look weak and lose people's respect." The second says, "When a person I respect admits her mistakes, I end up respecting her more." Isn't it amazing how you can know a fact but think you're the only one on the planet that it doesn't apply to?

Let's imagine that you lost your cool and ridiculed a worker in front of everyone. You can say you're sorry in two ways. No matter what words you use, the first kind of sorry means, "I'm sorry because it made *me* look like an idiot." The only thing you regret is the damage you did to yourself.

The second kind of sorry means, "I'm sorry because I embarrassed *you,* hurt *you,* and didn't treat *you* with the respect you deserve." You realize, regret, and admit the damage you did to the other person. You don't need to tell someone which sorry you mean—she knows from the way you say it.

When you're wrong, say it. Doing that may temporarily streak your self-image, but it polishes the image others see.

BE NICE

It's unusual to reach a day's end without getting hit with a negative remark from a teacher, coach, friend, sibling, or par-

LOOK, KID, IT'S NO BIG DEAL. YOU GO UP, COLLECT SOME MOON ROCKS, YOU COME BACK. JUST FOLLOW THE INSTRUCTION BOOKS.

ent. Some days you start to wonder if there's a note on your forehead: "Rip on me—I like it." You can create for your co-workers an oasis of praise in an often-cruel world. Here are some nice things to say and do:

Affirmation. Declare what's true. You affirm someone when you tell her what's true about herself: "You're a punctual person"; "You think clearly under pressure"; "You juggle chainsaws better than anyone I know." Since most of us are frequently reminded of what we aren't, it's a real boost to hear good things about our talents and qualities.

Your affirmation will carry twice the power if you show her proof of your accusation: "I just saw how you handled that angry woman. You were quiet and friendly, and you showed her that you cared. When it comes to dealing with customers, you're a pro." She can't deny it—you've got her pegged.

Encouragement. Fill someone's heart with hope. Long

hours, a tough workload, problems with coworkers—these things and a hundred more can discourage people on the job. You can give a little hope with a kind word, a smile, a round of M&Ms, or a pat on the back. One of the best encouragements is to pitch in and help someone get the job done.

Appreciation. Thank someone for what she's done for you: "Thanks for carrying the box—you saved me an extra trip"; "You make my job much easier: I appreciate your hard work"; "Thanks for squashing that bug—my dad's stuck in traffic."

Get in the habit of writing notes. Spoken praise is often forgotten, but a short note of affirmation, encouragement, or appreciation makes it official. You mean what you say.

9

HOW TO START YOUR OWN BUSINESS AND MAYBE EVEN MAKE MONEY AT IT

Starting a business is both scary and exciting. It's also a big job. There are lots of books devoted solely to the topic. If after reading this chapter you think you have what it takes to launch a successful business, go to the library or bookstore and find out all you can.

FIND A NEED AND FILL IT

Every business is an example of someone discovering a need and getting paid to fill it. People need more food than they can raise in their gardens, so grocery stores fill the need. The car burns up the gasoline that was in the tank when you bought it; gas stations fill the tank. Parents sometimes like to go places without their children but can't leave them running loose at home: baby-sitters provide the solution.

Because of changes in the economy and people's life-styles, new needs are being created all the time. Here are some of our society's growing needs in the 1990s, along with some student businesses you can create to fill those needs.

People want things done faster and easier.

Rent a Chef. Hire yourself out to neighbors and friends of your parents who don't have time to cook and clean up the dishes but would like an excellent meal prepared in their own homes.

Dining to Go. Few restaurants can afford to hire a delivery person for takeout meals. Get exclusive delivery rights from several popular restaurants, then put together a menu featuring some of the dinner specialties of each restaurant. Mail the menu to houses in the neighborhood. If someone wants a meal from the menu, he is to call you by 6:00 P.M. to place the order. You order the meals from the restaurants, pick them up, and make your deliveries.

Really Fresh Foods. Make your own peanut butter, apple pies, cookies, or candies. Package and sell them to neighbors and local stores.

Personal Shopper. Some adults are too busy to stand in line at the supermarket or drive all over town looking for a vacuum cleaner part. You take care of all their shopping needs at a certain cost per trip.

Go-to-Town Errands. Same idea, but you'll run any errand:

pick up clothes at the cleaners, stand in line at the department of motor vehicles, take the dog to the vet, bail their son out of jail.

KidLimo. Be a kid driver: pick up the kids after school, drop one at the day-care center, take another to baseball practice, and accompany the third to the dentist (if she's a brat, take her there every day).

Dog Gone Walking. For busy people with little time to exercise their dogs, offer memberships to your daily dog walking service, with washing and brushing on Saturdays. Also offer pet sitting to owners who're going out of town.

All Sewn Up. Most people have a stack of clothes that need mending, altering, or a button replaced. Offer door-to-door service.

Two-Wheel Tune. Instead of hauling their bikes to the shop for tune-ups and flat repairs, your customers call you—you do the work at their home for less. Offer tune-ups, flat repairs, adjustments, and detailing. Offer to buy their old bikes; fix them up and sell for a profit.

Short-Order Servant. Hire yourself out as a butler, maid, server, or dishwasher for private parties. Advertise on bulletin boards in tennis, country, or yacht clubs.

Friday Flowers. Sell once-a-week flower delivery to homes. Buy the flowers from a wholesaler, arrange them for each of your clients, and deliver them to their homes every Friday. Provide arrangements for special occasions.

Wrap It Up. Offer in-the-home holiday gift wrapping. Customers provide the wrapping paper, ribbons, and tags; you put it all together.

Hired Pen. If you're a calligrapher, sell your penmanship to people who need to create or address invitations, Christmas cards, or nametags.

Other Ideas: gardening, caring for lawns, housecleaning, fish tank cleaning, window washing, pool cleaning, car detailing, doing auto maintenance, washing and ironing, house sitting, plant sitting (but never sit *on* them), Christmas light hanging, snow clearing, leaf raking.

People want things that bring order to their complex world.

Mr. Bills. Stop by your clients' houses once a week to organize their bills, write checks for them to sign, mail the payments, and file the statements. Balance their checkbooks each month, and organize their receipts for tax time.

Maximum Memories. Put together photo albums for people who take lots of pictures but never seem to have the time to organize them. Create scrapbooks for their children containing art and schoolwork.

Proper Places. Organize people's kitchens, drawers, desks, albums, videos, files, offices, closets, pantries, and garages. Charge a fee for each area; offer package deals and monthly maintenance contracts.

I Haul. If you have a pickup truck, offer to haul away garden debris, old appliances, and junk piles for a set price per load.

People want quality services for their children.

KidCrafts. Hold crafts classes for neighborhood kids after school, on weekends, or during the summer. Print a flier that tells parents the craft you'll be teaching each day and how much money the child has to bring to participate.

PlayCamp. Offer a daycamp experience for neighborhood kids at a local park. Do crafts, games, stories, and snacks.

Party Performances. Perform as a clown or magician for children's parties.

KidVids. Offer to videotape birthday parties, bar and bat mitzvahs, recitals, plays, and sporting events. If you don't have a camera, see if you can borrow or rent one from school or a camera store.

Summer Girl. Hire yourself to a family as a nanny for the summer. Look after the kids all day during weekdays, with weekends off. If you don't want to work full-time, split the job with a friend by working alternating days.

Professor Tutor. Tutor kids in subjects you enjoy.

People want good service at a reasonable cost.

Formal Flowers. Sell dance corsages and boutonnieres to your classmates. Design several arrangements, take pictures, and use the photos to take orders. Get the flowers from a wholesaler and fill your orders.

Shirt Factory. Design and print art on sweatshirts, T-shirts, polo shirts, and bandanas for school clubs and sports teams. Also look for customers among community organizations and sports leagues.

Just My Type. Type reports for high-school and college students.

Page by Page. If you have access to a computer, laser printer, and desktop publishing software, offer to create fliers and mailings for small businesses. Lots of people send out Christmas letters; design and print their letters for them.

ASK THE RIGHT QUESTIONS

Once you have a hot business idea, you need to ask some tough questions to make sure your idea will fly:

The Need

• What need does your business idea fill? If you can't describe it in one sentence, you're going to have a tough time selling your idea to others.

The Market

• Who are your potential customers?
• How many are there?
• Will you meet one of them, fall in love, get married, and raise a family?
• How are you going to advertise your product or service?

The Legal Stuff

• Will you need a business license?
• If you're making or handling food, will you need a permit from the health department? What about insurance? Will you need to collect sales tax?

The Commitment

• How many hours will you have to work before making a profit?

- Can you honestly afford the hours away from other priorities to make this business work?
- If everyone knew the quadratic formula, would the world be a safer place?

The Reward

- Why are you doing this?
- What do you think you'll learn?
- What are the worst aspects to the venture?
- How much money will you make per hour?

The Finances

- What will it take to make money? To answer that question, you'll have to do a budget listing all your income and expenses. Here are a few expense categories to consider:

Marketing: fliers, mailings, ads.

Equipment: big stuff—computer, lawn mower, video camera.

Supplies: stuff you use up—dog shampoo, paper, flowers, stamps.

Administration: business license, rent, phone bills, loan interest.

For example, here is a basic budget for a dog walking and washing service that you run during the summer.

BUDGET PROJECTION

For: Dog Gone Walking
Business: Provide dog walking and washing for busy owners
Period: 3 months (summer)

INCOME
daily walking service
($30 per month x 10 dogs x 3 months) . . . . $ 900
washing service
($2 per wash x 5 dogs per week x 12 weeks)   120

EXPENSES
marketing (fliers on doorsteps, at vets and pet stores)   50
equipment (plastic tub, leash, pooper scooper)   50
supplies (shampoo, brushes)   20
administration (pay parents for use of water and towels)   30

OUTCOME
Total Income 1,020
Total Expenses   150
Net Profit (total income minus total expenses) . . . . $ 870

Cash Flow

If you already had $150 in cash to cover the initial expenses in the budget above, you'd be ready for business. But if you have to borrow money to get a business started, you also should do what's called a *cash flow projection* to see how much you'll need and for how long.

A cash flow projection is really just a series of budgets, one for each month. Let's say you're starting a gardening business. The first month you figure you won't have any income (no customers yet), but lots of expenses (fliers, equipment purchases)—you're $200 in the hole.

	Month 1
Income:	0
Expenses:	200
Net profit:	(200)*
Cumulative:	**($200)**

The second month you pick up some customers, but you've still got to buy more equipment: you're in the hole $20 for that month, plus the $200 from the first month— $220.

	Month 1	Month 2
Income:	0	100
Expenses:	200	120
Net profit:	(200)	(20)
Cumulative:	($200)	**($220)**

---

*In financial stuff, people usually use parentheses for negative numbers instead of minus signs.

The third month you've got more customers—and you've finally paid for most of your equipment. You come out ahead for the month, but use the profits to pay off the debt. Now you're just $70 "in the red." The fourth month you finally pay off your debt and make $240 cumulative profit.

	Month 1	Month 2	Month 3	Month 4
Income:	0	100	230	350
Expenses:	200	120	80	40
Net profit:	(200)	(20)	150	310
Cumulative:	($200)	($220)	($ 70)	**$240**

-107-

Now you're ready to figure out a way to borrow $220 for three to four months.

Hope for the Best, Plan for the Worst

After you've done a budget, do another. This time, run a projection using the best possible conditions: excellent response to your marketing effort, good deals on supplies. Then do a third budget, using the worst numbers: fewer customers paying lower prices, higher business expenses. Together, the three budgets will give you a range of performance for your business.

PART THREE

IS ABOUT SAVING MONEY

10

YAZOFF SELLS PIGS
(OR HOW MONEY WORKS)

Virtually every book about money puts me to sleep. Not wanting to put you through the same experience, I've written a story about it. I hope it helps you to understand how this thing called money works. And if not . . . happy napping.

Yazoff raises pigs. He needs a horse. He goes to Hal the horse handler: "How many pigs for a horse?"

Hal: "I don't hawk horses for hogs, but I'll give you one horse for two llamas. You got any llamas?"

"Not on me, but I'll be back." Yazoff goes across town to Elena the llama dealer (two doors down from Ynes the Yamaha dealer). "How many pigs for two llamas?"

"Pshaah! I don't purchase pigs, but I'll swap you two llamas for a hundred pounds of pretzels. You got any pretzels?"

"Not on me, but I'll be back." Yazoff goes to Prudence the pretzelmaker. "How many pigs for a hundred pounds of pretzels?"

"I sell the pretzels in forty-pound bags, two pigs for a bag."

"I need two and a half bags."

"I only sell whole bags—that'll be six pigs."

Yazoff goes home, brings back six pigs, then makes three trips to Elena the llama dealer to deliver the three bags of pret-

THE U.S. PIG POPULATION IN 1989: 55.3 MILLION.

zels. He trades the pretzels for the llamas; she throws in two unhealthy hens for the extra twenty pounds of pretzels. Yazoff trades the llamas for the horse. Result: six pigs and a whole day of trading for a horse and two sick chickens.

The drag about bartering was, you couldn't buy anything unless you had something the seller wanted. If all you had were pigs or pretzels, and the seller didn't want pigs or pretzels, you'd have to find someone who did. And you had to do it fast: pigs and all other livestock must be fed; pretzels and other kinds of foods go stale. What was needed was an object that was easily carried, didn't die or spoil, and was considered valuable by most people. And that was gold.

Good as Gold

Gold was hard to mine and mint, so it held value. Governments began to mint gold into small, uniform disks called coins,* which were easy to weigh and carry. The greatest thing about the use of gold coins in trading was that it separated the buying from the selling. If you had plenty of food at the moment, you could sell your llamas now and buy the food a few months later. Another rare metal, silver, was also used for coins.

Promises in Writing

Paper money started out as IOU notes. If a government was short on gold or silver for minting (not the candy), it might pay its workers in promissory notes. A note could be exchanged for—and therefore was as good as—the amount of gold listed on it. But unlike IOU notes, which promise to pay the money to a certain person only, these notes were made out to

ALL THE GOLD EVER MINED WOULD FIT IN ONE OIL TANKER

...AND IF I GET BACK, I PROMISE TO PAY YOU!

---

*Not to be confused with gold foil-wrapped chocolates called mints.

"bearer"—anyone in possession of the note could exchange it at the government bank. As long as people believed in the government's ability to make good on the promise, they treated the notes just like gold coins.

As America became a big-time world power in this century, the U.S. government began severing the relationship between gold and money. It stopped minting regular coins out of gold and silver and stopped printing notes that could be exchanged for the stuff. Now a dollar's value lies in the fact that America is a stable and diverse country, and you'll always be able to buy and sell freely with millions of others who agree to the same value for the currency, so it's okay. It's kind of a wild idea, but that's how the system works. The dollar now has value because we believe it does.

Personal Exchange Rate

Money is worth whatever you believe it to be—you choose the exchange rate. Your wallet contains time, energy, talent, integrity, and freedom. If you want money, you have to pay for it with one or more of these valuables.

For example, Marla cuts her hours and $100 weekly paycheck in half so she can volunteer at an AIDS hospice. To her, the volunteer time was worth more than $50. Her brother Jason makes $50 in one hour selling crack to junior highers. To him, $50 is worth more than the risk to his freedom, reputation—and the lives of his "customers." They live in the same house and deal in the same currency, but their valuations of money are very different.

You can tell how much a person values something by what he's willing to spend to get it: high price, high value. Every time you get a job or make an investment, you have to price the deal according to your exchange rate: What will this investment do to my values—my bottom line? Lots of people pay exorbitant prices for their wealth. They swindle themselves, and when they want their values back, there's no one to sue.

I bring this up because I don't want all these investment and money management ideas to artificially inflate your value of money. Some teenagers make the accumulation of money their primary goal. That's too expensive.

It's important to set financial goals and invest wisely, but it's just one part of your bottom line. When it comes to handling money, it's okay to get good; just don't get crazy.

"MONEY OFTEN COSTS TOO MUCH."—Ralph Waldo Emerson

11

MONEY ADVICE VIRTUALLY NO ONE FOLLOWS

Here are four pieces of advice to help you earn more money with your investments. They're really very simple and logical, yet most adults don't follow them. And that's part of the reason adults have so many money problems. Following this advice takes patience and discipline, but it pays off in big ways: more money, more control over your future, and more freedom to carry out your dreams.

INVEST IN THINGS THAT GO UP IN VALUE

Every dollar you spend is an investment; what you buy with it goes up or down in value. The moment you buy a stereo, cd, pair of shoes, or sunglasses, you lose money because you can never sell those items for what you paid. You lose that money when you buy the item, and you also lose the money you would have gained by investing in something that goes up in value.

Two Investments

Let's say you and your friend, Siegfried, each have $500 in cash and go shopping for stereos. He decides to buy one for $500. If he needed to get his money out of it at the end of the year, he could probably sell it to someone's kid brother for $300. His cost for stereo music for the year: $200. In other words, his stereo *depreciated* (went down in value) $200.

But you decided you could survive on your clock radio, and instead invested your $500 at the bank in a one-year certificate of deposit (CD) account yielding about 8 percent. At the end of the year you have $500 in principal and about $40 in interest. Siegfried lost out on this $40 opportunity. This $40 *opportunity cost* plus the $200 depreciation actually makes him $240 poorer than you at the end of the year.

In five years his $500 stereo investment is now worth $100; yours is $735 if you kept reinvesting in one-year CDs paying 8 percent—a gain of $235. The true cost of Siegfried's stereo in relation to your investment:

After 5 Years

Depreciation	$400
Opportunity Cost	235
TOTAL COST OF SIEGFRIED'S STEREO	$635

Cut Down on Downs

There's nothing wrong with buying a stereo. But you've got to realize that when you buy a stereo, car, shoes, or just about any consumer item, it goes down in value. If you sell it, you can't get as much as you paid for it. When it goes down in value, you lose money. Every time you invest in something that goes up in value, you make money.

The dozens of little things you spend money for each month add up to lots of money. Right now, when you don't have to pay for rent, home insurance, grocery bills, and medical expenses, you can be saving a substantial percentage of your income. If you really want to save money, avoid spending it on things that go down in value.

Fill Up on Ups

One of the best ways to invest money is to spend it on things that will help you make more money. Buy a snow blower, tool set, car-detailing equipment, or word processor—then clear driveways, fix stereos, detail cars, or type papers for others. If the initial investment is too steep, team up with a friend and start a partnership. Work together or alternate the days that each is entitled to use the equipment. For business ideas, see chapter 9.

Investments That *Can* Go Up

- money market accounts
- certificates of deposit
- mutual funds
- stocks
- bonds
- gold
- coins
- classic cars
- business equipment
- real estate education

Investments That *Usually* Go Down

- stereos
- clothes
- shoes
- Chicken McNuggets
- Madonna albums
- new cars
- used cars
- TVs
- surfboards
- video rentals

$15 per month $?

$15 per month $186

NEVER BORROW MONEY TO PAY FOR THINGS THAT GO DOWN IN VALUE

Let's go back to the stereo illustration. When your friend Winona saw Siegfried's stereo, she decided to rush out the next day and buy the same model. But Winona had only $50, which she used as a down payment. The store gracefully arranged to lend her $450 at 18 percent interest, which she could pay back in twelve monthly payments of $41.25. Winona is losing money in three (count 'em) exciting ways:

Depreciation: Her stereo, like Siegfried's, is losing value.

Opportunity Cost: Her money could be *earning* interest instead.

Finance Charge: She pays interest for the use of the money.

So here's what the stereo really costs her:

	After 1 Year	After 5 Years
1. Depreciation	$200	$400
2. Opportunity Cost*	15	217
3. Finance Charge	45	45
TOTAL COST OF WINONA'S STEREO	$260	$662

At the end of five years your two friends sell their stereos for $100 each. Siegfried's five years of stereo sound cost him $635 in money and lost opportunity; the same stereo cost Winona $662 in money and lost opportunity. You made $235.

---

*This assumes that she could have put the initial $50 in a savings account paying 5.25 percent interest compounded daily, added $41.25 per month to the account during the first year, and then invested the total in 8 percent CDs for the next four years. Some restrictions apply. Rates subject to change. Substantial penalty for early withdrawal. See your local banker. An equal opportunity lender. Member, FDIC.

Up a Down Escalator

If you're trying to save money for a car, a stereo—anything—don't borrow money for something that depreciates in value. While the bank is paying you 5 percent or 7 percent or 9 percent interest on the money you lend it (with your savings account), you're paying the bank—or some other lender—15 percent to 20 percent interest for the right to borrow it back. Does this sound ridiculous to you? It should! It's like trying to go up the down escalator.

But most people don't follow this advice. They buy on credit and lose in interest charges some or all of the gain in their appreciating investments. It's the American way. For more on the thrills and chills of borrowing, see chapter 15.

INVEST IN THINGS THAT OUTPERFORM INFLATION

Even if you invest in something that goes up in value, inflation can still make you lose money on it.

Inflation is the tendency of prices to rise, making a dollar worth less. A 5 percent annual inflation rate might cause a loaf of bread that cost $1.00 last year to run you $1.05: same number of slices, same silly face on the wrapper, just five cents more to buy. So if you have $100 invested for a year in a savings account that yields 5 percent, you now have $105. Last year your $100 could have bought 100 loaves of bread. This year your $105 will buy you the same thing: 100 loaves of bread. You didn't lose money, but you also didn't gain any. You have the same *purchasing power* you started with.

But suppose inflation is at 8 percent. Your money, making 5 percent at the bank, is worth 3 percent less than last year in terms of what you can buy with it. If you hid the $100 under

...YOUR SAVINGS ACCOUNT?

your bed, you lost $8. In countries such as Brazil, which suffered a 1,200 percent annual inflation rate in recent years, your $100 in currency could be worth $1 within a month! Few people even bothered to keep money in savings. The best "investment" was to spend the cash before it became worthless.

Because of inflation, the worst savings investment is putting your money in a piggy bank (despite how good it looks in your bedroom). The value of your money hidden in the envelope stuffed in the sock beneath the third dresser drawer will shrink by the rate of inflation (the money, not the sock).

In 1980 and 1981 inflation went "double digits"—10 percent and higher. If it heads that high again, you'll have to scramble to beat it.

MAKE AN APPRECIATING INVESTMENT EVERY MONTH

Maybe you're planning to start investing as soon as you have "enough." But unless you win the lottery or rob a bank, you'll never suddenly have one big chunk to invest. Instead, you have to save up small amounts every month for several months before you can make a "big" investment. Invest your first amount today.

You're Rich

The majority of an adult's income goes to pay for housing, utilities, medical expenses, and the daily costs of living—toothpaste, toilet paper, TV repair, and the *Time* subscription. Chances are, you don't have any of these expenses. You pay

"HE WHO GATHERS MONEY LITTLE BY LITTLE MAKES IT GROW."—Solomon

for only a small portion of your food. If you don't pay for a car, gas, or insurance, you have it easy. And if your folks pay for most or all of your clothing, you have it made.

In fact, you may be richer than your parents in terms of *discretionary income*—the money that's left after all the necessary bills are paid. Whether your income is an allowance, a minimum wage job, baby-sitting money, or a birthday check from your Aunt Elba, you can afford to invest a greater percentage of it. While most adults struggle to put away 5 percent of their income, lots of teenagers can save 70 percent.

If you have a regular monthly take-home income of $250, put away $175 every month. If you get a $25 allowance, put away $18. If you have an irregular income from baby-sitting or odd jobs, put away 70 percent of every check you receive.

12

BANK STUFF

Banks and savings and loans are good at coming up with fancy names for their accounts, names like "Advantage Plus Mega-Money Super Savings Certificate Account." But most of their accounts fit into one of four basic categories:

• *Basic Savings* accounts (sometimes called passbook accounts) have little or no minimum balance and pay a minimum interest. *Advantages:* you can withdraw your money whenever you want (no minimum deposit period), and you earn more interest than if you hid the money in that secret place near your bed (shh). *Disadvantage:* the interest you earn barely beats inflation in good years and falls way behind in bad ones.

• *Basic Checking* accounts don't pay interest, but they don't cost you anything as long as you keep a minimum balance. If your balance drops below the minimum, the bank charges you a monthly fee. Some banks also charge you a few cents per check.

• *Money Market* checking and savings accounts pay better interest than basic savings accounts, with the rate rising according to the amount of the balance. They also have higher minimum balances, usually $1,000 or more. They usually offer ATM (automatic teller machine) cards, which are nice to

have if you're shy and don't like talking to human tellers. ATM cards also make night and weekend banking possible for both shy and outgoing customers.

• *Certificates of Deposit* (CDs) are guarantees that you will let the bank keep a certain amount of money (generally $1,000 or more) for a certain period (one month to ten years) in exchange for higher interest. If you need your money before the CD matures, you pay a stiff penalty. Obviously, the more money you give the bank and the longer it stays there, the more interest will be guaranteed. Some banks offer $500

CDs, which makes them a good investment possibility for lots of teenagers.

Juggling Interest

Before you go shopping for a bank investment, you need to know how banks figure interest. There are two kinds: the kind you pay, and the kind you receive. Here's how it works when you're on the receiving end.

Let's say that while walking out of a store, you hold open the door for a man. He's amazed at your politeness and hands you $10,000 as a gesture of his thanks. When the crowd revives you from fainting, you remember the $10,000 in your pocket and race to the bank. You deposit the money into an account at a 9 percent annual percentage rate (apr), com-

INCLUDING INTEREST AND PRINCIPLE AND
SUBTRACTING OUR USUAL BANKING FEES,
SERVICE FEES, PARKING FEES, AND MY FEES
YIELDS YOU A BALANCE OF... EIGHTY-FIVE CENTS.

pounded monthly. The "9 percent" part sounds good; the "compounded" part sounds like something for warts. But you make your deposit and go off to tell your friends what happened. The bank puts your money into a little envelope with your name on it and hides it in the vault.

On the first day of the next month, a little man named Harold takes his calculator into the vault to count the money in your envelope: $10,000 (phew!)—which he multiplies by three-fourths of 1 percent (.0075). Your question at this point should be, Why did Harold pick *that* number?

The answer is, it's one-twelfth of 9 percent—one-month's worth of your interest rate. When he multiplies your $10,000 by .0075, his calculator shows that the bank owes you $75 in interest for the first month. Then he takes $75 out of a little green money bag he carries and places it in your envelope.

The next month Harold is at it again. He counts the money in your envelope—$10,075—multiplies it by .0075, then puts $75.56 into your envelope. He does this every month for the year. "Compounded monthly" means Harold takes his calculator into the vault once a month. (Actually, one time he was sick so Hector did it.)

At the end of the year, you withdraw your money. Out of the vault comes your envelope: your original $10,000 plus $938 in interest. Wait a minute: 9 percent of $10,000 is $900—you were overpaid $38. Not really. The extra $38 was the interest you received on the *interest* (called compounded interest). Your $10,000 earned $938 in interest in one year.

Or, in moneytalk, your principal of $10,000 yielded 9.38 percent for a return on investment of $938.

Let's say you put your money in an account paying 9 percent interest compounded yearly. Twelve months after you deposited the money, Harold takes his calculator into the vault to figure your interest: $10,000 × .09 (12 months' worth of interest) = $900. Your yield: 9.00 percent. This is not only a worse deal for you but really boring for Harold.

The way to compare interest accounts is by their yields— what you get out of them. Here is a comparison of one-year yields on $10,000 at a 9 percent annual percentage rate:*

	interest	yield
compounded *yearly*	$900	9.00%
compounded *monthly*	938	9.38%
compounded *daily*	942	9.42%

I'M HAROLD.
I'M UNEMPLOYED.

Before we go on, I feel obligated to tell you the truth: Harold doesn't go into the vault to count your money. Two reasons. First, there's no one named Harold at your bank—he

---

*Based on a 360-day year.

was replaced by a computer several years ago (I know . . . it's sad) that automatically calculates your interest at each compounding. Second, your money isn't in the vault. The bank loaned it to a woman named Rita who is opening the Reptile Emporium down the street (no lie). Rita is paying the bank 14 percent interest for the $10,000. After paying your interest, the bank still makes 5 percent on the deal.*

Which brings up the other type of interest: the kind you pay. The interest is just a fee you pay for the privilege of using the lender's money. Rita's $10,000 loan at 14 percent annual interest must be repaid in one year. At the end of the year she gives the bank the principal (the original $10,000) plus $1,400 simple interest. In other words, the interest is calculated once—there's no compounding as in a savings account. Most lenders—banks, credit card issuers, retail stores—charge simple interest.

For more information on receiving interest (yes, yes, yes), read on. For more on paying interest (no, no, no), see chapter 15.

MAKING MONEY AT THE BANK

Bank CDs are one of the best investments you can make as a teenager. Your money is insured in case the bank goes belly up (which banks do occasionally), and the guaranteed interest rate is higher than a savings account. And because your money is locked up for the prescribed time period, you can't spend it on a new wardrobe in a fit of insanity. If you have

---

*Okay, okay . . . there's more to it than this—the length of the reptilean loan, whether it's being paid off monthly or all at once, and so on. But this is just an *illustration*. Can we go on?

money sitting in a savings account or piggy bank, stick it in a CD and start earning some real interest.

Problem

What if you don't have the $500 or $1,000 minimum to open a CD?

Three Solutions

1. Sweating. It's really tough to make an investment return* that outpaces inflation if you don't have this kind of money. Save your allowance, store up the birthday checks, work a few extra hours—and above all, spend less.

2. Pooling. You're not the only one with this problem. Find one or two friends with some money to invest. Put in identical amounts and set up the account so that each of you has to sign for the money. At the end of the period divide the principal (original investment) and interest evenly. (This is just a smaller version of a mutual fund.)

3. Bumping. Hang out in front of the bank. If a rich elderly woman walks out carrying a handful of cash, accidentally bump into her and see if she drops it. Just kidding—bumping is like pooling, except you're just using someone else's money to bump you into the "big leagues." A relative with money in the bank may be willing to let you use a few hundred dollars of it for a bump if you agree to pay her the portion of the interest that's hers. For example, if she puts in $700 to bump your $300 for a $1,000 CD, pay her 70 percent of the yield. Keep track of her money and repay it when your savings can stand on its own.

---

*Refresher course: *return* = what you earn from your investment, in dollars or as a percentage of the original investment (also called *yield*); *ungulate* = a hoofed animal.

IN 1929, THE U.S. SHRANK THE SIZE OF ITS PAPER MONEY BY 31 PERCENT.

Minor Difficulties

According to the government, a contractual agreement made with a minor can't be enforced against you. These laws are designed to protect you from being hurt by bad deals. But they also keep lots of banks and other businesses from entering into legitimate deals with you. For example, if an adult overdraws her checking account by $500 and refuses to pay back the money, the bank can take her to court and make her pay. If you're a minor and do the same thing, the court won't recognize the agreement between you and the bank as a legal contract—the bank loses its money.

This doesn't mean banks can't do business with you—they just don't have the law to back them up if you go astray. So most banks won't go very far out of their way to help you. On rare occasions, if your mom or dad is a very good customer of the bank (read, keeps loads of money there), a bank officer may be willing to let you open a checking or money market account.

More likely, banks will require that a parent or guardian be a signer on the account. That way they can go after the adult if you go on a spending spree with your checkbook. Many banks tend to be easier on the age restriction with CDs, allowing you to open one without a cosigner. Of course, they're holding all your money, so it's no great gesture on their part.

It's strange, but that's too great a gesture for some. A few banks want nothing to do with you until you reach eighteen. They won't even let you open a checking or money market account *with* a cosigner.

My advice is, don't play with them. Hunt around until you find a bank that's willing to treat you as a young adult, and do your business there. If the people treat you right, tell your friends to open accounts there, too. If the service and the respect you receive from the bank justify it, write a letter to the bank's manager or president.

A few bankers know the value of having teenage customers. The rest will find out that your $50 or $500 account will be a $5,000 or $50,000 account someday, and you've got strong loyalty—and a good memory.

Minor Triumphs

Credit unions are not reluctant to serve teenage customers. Some offer virtually all the services of a bank, with little of the age discrimination. Some credit unions are open only to employees of a certain company, government office, or industry. A few are open to any worker who wishes to join.

If you're working, you may be able to join a credit union on

YOUR BUTLER'S BANK CHECK

A check is an IOU note from you to the person you write it to. Originally, checks were just handwritten notes: "Dear Biff's Bank: Please give my butler, Bernard, $100 from my account."

Bernard would take your signed note to Biff's Bank. Someone would check the signature on the note to see that it matched the one in your file and give Bernard the cash from your account.

To make things easier, banks began to print up standard forms for these IOU notes, putting your account number, name, address, and so forth, right on the form. This makes it possible for Bernard to "cash" the check at his bank: Tish's Trust and Savings (TT&S). When he does, the bank keeps the check and gives him $100. Then it trades the check with the Federal Reserve Bank (the bank for banks), which gives TT&S $100 by depositing that much into TT&S's account.

Then the Federal Reserve Bank trades the check with Biff's Bank by giving it the check and deducting $100 from its account. Biff's Bank trades with you: you get the canceled (and well-traveled) check, and it takes $100 from your account. Everybody is even. Until you bounce a check.

Everything goes fine until the Federal Reserve Bank wants to swap your bank the check for the $100, and your bank sees that you don't have enough money to cover it. Your bank tells the Federal Reserve Bank, "No deal!" The Federal Reserve Bank gives the check back to Tish's Trust and Savings and takes the $100 back out of its account. TT&S calls your butler and demands the $100 back. Bernard returns the $100 and goes to you with the bad check. This time you give him cash.

your own. If your mother or father is a member, the union may also let you join. Because they're nonprofit institutions and don't have to pay the taxes banks do, they're able to offer higher yielding basic savings, money market, and CD accounts; they can also provide car and personal loans to their members at lower-than-bank interest rates. Many also offer VISA and MasterCard accounts (even to creditworthy seventeen-year-olds).

Then there's the Young Americans Bank in Denver, Colorado. This bank knows how to treat you right! In fact, you have to be *under* twenty-one to do business there. It offers savings and checking accounts as well as small business loans for young entrepreneurs. Anyone under twenty-one can open an account if you have an adult sponsor who will vouch for you (and pay off your debt if you spin out of control). Teenagers and kids all over the U.S. have started banking there. A MasterCard with a $100 credit limit is available to bank customers with at least six months of well-behaved savings or checking account activity. To find out more or to open an account, contact: Young Americans Bank, 250 Steele Street, Denver CO 80206; (303) 321-2265.

13

MUTUAL FUNDS EXPLAINED PRETTY CLEARLY

IN 1988, U.S. INDIVIDUALS HAD $298.3 BILLION INVESTED IN MONEY MARKET FUNDS.

Here's your chance to own stock in dozens of companies! A mutual fund is a collection of stocks, bonds, or other kinds of investments bought by a bunch of people and managed by professionals. It's kind of like a club: everyone who puts money in the fund owns portions of every investment in the fund.

Let's say you have $500 to invest. You could buy 100 shares of a stock trading at $5 per share, but that's putting all your eggs in one basket. You could spread things around by buying 20 shares in five different companies, but the stock-broker will charge you about $200 to buy them for you!

But if you pooled your money with nine other people with $500 each, your group would have a fund with $5,000 to invest. Then you could buy several stocks and spread the risks and costs among you. Your share is 10 percent of every stock owned by the group: if one company doesn't do well, the performance of the others can offset the loss. That is how a mutual fund works.

With a mutual fund, thousands of people invest varying amounts, and professional managers choose which invest-ments will be best for everyone in the group. Since the fund manager often has millions of dollars to work with, he usually invests in 50 to 100 different securities (stocks, bonds, etc.).

Investing in a Mutual Fund

Nearly all mutual funds are sold directly by the investment companies and financial institutions that manage them. If you decide to buy shares in a fund, you'll have to send a check for at least the minimum amount, typically $250 to $1,000. After that, you can usually make additional investments of $250 or more, as often as you like.

You need to be eighteen to invest in a mutual fund by yourself. If you're not, you can ask an adult to buy the shares for you as a "gift," under the Uniform Gift to Minors Act (UGMA). The investment is yours, but your trustee (the adult) is legally responsible for the transactions. The fund office will tell you how to do this.

If you're buying a *load* fund, you'll also have to pay a commission to the fund manager—from 3 percent to 8.5 percent, depending on the fund. There's generally no charge when you sell. (Okay, just to be different, some load funds charge an "exit fee" when you sell, but nothing when you buy. A few get you at both ends.) A no-load fund won't charge you a sales fee. Some funds have penalties if you sell your shares back to them too quickly.

A good source of mutual fund information is *Money* magazine, which tracks the best performing funds each month. The magazine also tells you about the various kinds of funds: some good for long-term investment, others good for risky short-term buys, and still others good for people who pay lots of taxes. The listings also include toll-free numbers you can call to receive information. Annually, *Money, Business Week,*

IN 1988, U.S. INDIVIDUALS HAD $417.5 BILLION INVESTED IN STOCK AND BOND FUNDS.

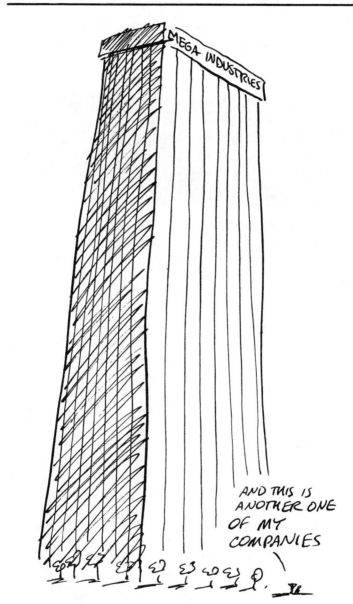

and other magazines print ratings for all major mutual funds to help you compare funds and learn about their managers' strategies.

OTHER INVESTMENTS I WON'T MAKE YOU READ ABOUT

Lots of other investments are out there, but for various reasons most aren't well suited for teenage investors. If you're interested in pursuing any of these, be sure to learn all you can before spending any money.

Stocks

When you own a share of stock, you own a portion of the company. If the company does well and the stock value goes up, you can sell your share for a *capital gain*. If the company has healthy profits, it may set aside a portion of them to send to each shareholder in the form of a *dividend*. Those are the two main ways of making money with stock.

To buy stock, you have to use a middleman called a stockbroker who charges you a commission for his work. The minimum commission (for the smallest orders) is generally about $40 or more. If you buy $500 worth of stock in one company, you have to earn 8 percent on the investment just to cover this commission. When you sell it, you'll pay another $40. That means your stock has to rise in value by 16 percent or pay huge dividends just for you to break even! You can see that small investments in stocks are really expensive. Stock mutual funds are a better deal for smaller investors.

Bonds

Bonds are loans to companies and governments. With most bonds, you lend the issuer $1,000 for a certain time period—up to thirty years. The issuer sends you the interest every year and gives you the $1,000 back at the end of the loan. Bonds are good for people who need to earn a regular income from their investments to cover expenses. But you already have income from an allowance or part-time job, so you're better off with investments that grow bigger—growth funds and CDs.

And More . . .

Gold, silver, collectibles, real estate, futures trading, and options. These instruments either require too much money to get going, or are too complicated to try to explain here. If you're a millionaire whiz kid, you should be able to find information on these investments at the library.

WASHINGTON MUST HAVE THROWN A SPANISH PESO ACROSS THE POTOMAC (THE U.S. DIDN'T MINT SILVER DOLLARS UNTIL 1792).

14

HOW TO GET TO YOUR
FIRST $500 AND BEYOND

There's no way for me to know what investments are best for your situation, but I can tell you what's good for most teenagers.

1. Go for growth. Your number one investment goal is to make your money grow. Right now you have few expenses compared to your income. But soon you'll be paying for cars, education, furniture, entertainment, clothes, food, housing, medical expenses, and a thousand other things that will obliterate your paycheck so fast it will make your wallet spin. Make the right investments now and your money will grow substantially until you *really* need it.

2. Take some risks. Mutual funds that grow quickly are risky investments. But more than just about any other age group, you can probably afford to take those risks. Your salary will only increase as you get older, and you can replenish what you lose much faster because you can put into savings the money that adults have to put into housing, food, medical, and other living expenses. At the same time, you want to keep at least half your savings in insured, guaranteed investments such as bank CDs and money market funds. If the money is

your ticket to college, limit your risky investments to one-third to one-fourth of your savings.

3. Don't bother with income investments. Some people (retired folks, for example) invest in bonds, "high-yield" stocks and mutual funds so that they'll get interest and dividend checks in the mail. They use this income to pay their regular living expenses. But you don't have very many living expenses—and the ones you have can easily be covered with a part-time job or even your allowance. Invest in things that go up in value; if they pay you interest or a dividend, reinvest it immediately and keep your money growing.

4. Lock it up. Unless you're making loan payments, large cash reserves aren't critical. Most adults try to keep a large reserve in a money market savings account in case they have a major emergency or are out of work for a few months. It's different with you. If you lose your job, you probably won't be evicted. It's best to keep your money locked into investments that you won't be tempted to invade every day.

Here are some investment ideas to help you get to the first critical levels of investing.

GETTING TO $500

• If you don't have a regular job, do whatever you can to *make* at least $15 per week for a year. Deposit $10 *every* week into a savings account. Use the remaining $5 per week as your spending allowance.

- If you have a job, deposit 70 percent of every paycheck in a savings account. If you can get by without junk food every week and new clothes every month, put aside 80 percent. If you're desperate, go for 90 percent.
- Deposit *all* of every birthday check in the account.
- Don't borrow money.
- *Don't make withdrawals from the account* (that's why it's called savings). Money for Christmas gifts and other special expenses need to come out of your spending allowance.

When You've Arrived at $500

- Put your first $500 in a CD. If interest rates are rising, go for a short-term CD (one or three months) and keep reinvesting it in a higher-paying CD each time it matures. If interest rates are falling, lock it away for a year at a time.

• If you can't find a CD that will accept $500, pool or bump your $500 up to $1,000 (see chapter 12).

GETTING TO $1,000

• If you don't have a regular job, work to make $25 per week for seven months. Deposit $18 every week; use the remaining $7 to spend as your allowance and to save for Christmas and birthday gifts.

• If you have a job, keep putting away 70 percent of every paycheck. Increase your savings percentage by one point for every 5 percent raise you get. For example, if your raise takes you from $5.00 to $5.50 per hour—a 10 percent raise—increase your savings percentage by two points, to 72 percent. The raise will still boost your spending allowance, plus your savings will grow even faster.*

• Start studying mutual fund investments. Pick up copies of *Money* magazine and follow its fund reports. Call the funds you like and ask for information. (Look for funds that will accept a $500 investment.)

When You've Arrived at $1,000

$500: Invest the new $500 in a carefully researched mutual fund. (If you're under eighteen, you'll need to set up a trustee arrangement with a trusted adult.)

$500 (plus interest): Reinvest your original $500 plus the interest in a CD.

---

*To calculate the percentage of your pay raise, divide the amount of the raise by what you used to make. A 25¢ pay raise from $4.50 per hour is .25 ÷ 4.50 = .06, or 6%.

THE U.S. $500, $1,000, $5,000, AND $10,000 NOTES WERE REMOVED FROM CIRCULATION IN 1969.

I THOUGHT IF I BOUGHT ENOUGH LOTTERY TICKETS I COULD COME UP WITH AT LEAST ONE $2000.ºº WINNER.....

GETTING TO $1,500

• If you don't have a regular job, work to earn $35 per week for five months. Deposit $25 in a savings account every week; use the $10 as a spending allowance.

• With a regular job, continue to put away your percentage with every paycheck. Keep increasing your savings percentage by adding half the percentage of each raise.

• Continue to follow the progress of your mutual fund and other funds you're interested in.

When You've Arrived at $1,500

$500: Put the new $500 in a CD.

$500 (plus interest): Keep reinvesting the original CD funds.

$500 (more or less): Hold onto your original mutual fund.

GETTING TO $2,000

• If you still don't have a regular job, stop and marvel at how far you've come without it. Now up the ante: $50 a week for three and one-half months. Deposit $35; keep $15. If you can't pull this off, put away 70 percent to 75 percent of whatever you bring in.

• If you have a regular job, keep putting away your savings percentage and increasing it with your raises.

When You've Arrived at $2,000

$1,000 (more or less): Add the newest $500 to your mutual fund, or invest in another fund.

$1,000 (plus interest): Keep reinvesting the CD funds.

GETTING TO $3,000

• Continue to put 70 percent or more of your income into savings. As long as you don't have to pay for most of your housing, food, and medical bills, you can afford to build up large savings.

• Pay close attention to the progress of your investments.

U.S. DOLLARS HAVE BEEN MADE OUT OF GOLD, SILVER, PEWTER, AND PAPER.

When You've Arrived at $3,000

It's more of the same strategy. Invest for growth; keep at least half in insured investments. If you remove money from CDs, put it in a money market account until you do something else with it—it will pay you better interest than a basic savings or checking account, and it's safer than your sock drawer.

If you're saving for college a few years away, consider locking up money in longer-term CDs.

When your income is big enough, consider making regular monthly investments into a mutual fund rather than waiting to make a yearly investment.

PART FOUR

IS ABOUT SPENDING MONEY

15

HOW TO BORROW MONEY WITHOUT TOTALLY MESSING UP YOUR LIFE

The best advice for borrowing money is this: *don't*.

For many people, borrowing has become a way of life. The temptation is fierce. By paying with cash, you could barely afford a $150 stereo; by making monthly payments of just $30, you can own an $800 system. And instead of slaving away your summer earning money for a new wardrobe this fall, you can charge the clothing on a credit card and pay off the balance over several months.

It seems magical. You can own things you could never afford to buy with cash. But the truth is, you don't own them.

When you buy something on installment (make monthly payments), you don't really own it—the lender does. And the firm makes a killing by letting you use it. Many stores and credit card companies charge you 20 percent (or more) annual interest on the money you owe them—that's *two to four times* the amount your bank is probably paying you for the use of your money. So while your $500 savings account earns about $25 in interest in one year, the $500 you owed during that year cost you $100 in interest.

Borrowing money to pay for things that depreciate is like trying to go up a down elevator.

In essence, someone with unpaid credit card balances is lending her savings account to the bank so it can loan her own money to her and charge her for the privilege (think about that one). As I mentioned earlier, borrowing money to pay for things that depreciate is like trying to go up a down escalator.

Car Loans

Getting a loan to buy a new car is especially silly. Most new cars lose at least 10 percent of their value the moment you drive them off the lot. So the 10 percent down payment you made pays for that new car smell, nothing else.

And then there's the interest on the loan. By the time the car is paid off, you will have paid from 15 percent to 30 percent more than if you had paid cash. The only good news is that most cars depreciate more slowly after four or five years, so your investment probably won't get any worse after that (unless it starts falling apart by then).

That's if you hang around long enough to pay it off—most people want a new car before they've finished paying for the old one. If you sell the car, you'll probably get enough for it to pay off the loan balance and *maybe* enough left over to cover another down payment. But car prices have gone up, so your monthly payments (and insurance) also rise. That raise you just got will come in handy.

Now you're on the treadmill that car dealers and banks want you on. You're addicted to the smell of new cars, the monthly car payment becomes a fact of life for you, and it saps up so much of your income that you can't save enough to pay cash the next time around. It's a downward spiral.

So earn your money, pay cash for a reliable used car, and use the money you save in interest to pay for a trip to Europe. And while you're in Germany, remember to send postcards to the friends working all summer just to make payments on cars that were *made* there. (For more on car buying, see chapter 18.)

CAR LEASES

Car loans are such bad investments that it's actually cheaper sometimes just to rent the car for two to five years, with an option to buy. This rental with an option to buy is called a closed-end lease. If you decide to keep the car, your payments will count toward the purchase. If you don't want it, you can give it back to the dealer or the bank and walk away. All the money you spent in payments is gone forever, and you may be charged for extra mileage and wear.

In the end, a car lease is like a car loan. If you want to drive around in a car that a bank bought *for* you, you're probably going to lose money.

Investment Borrowing

Buying on credit is a smart investment only when the thing you buy will *increase* in value. If the amount of its appreciation (increase) is greater than the cost of the loan, it may be worth

borrowing for. Here are some instances where borrowing may be wise:

Business investment. Let's say you're really good at desktop publishing. You know you could produce fliers, brochures, and newsletters for several clients if you could buy a computer and software. If your business plan shows that you could afford the interest on a loan and still make a healthy profit, borrowing money may be a smart business investment. Depending on your tax situation, the interest on such a loan may be deductible as a business expense.

Education. A good education is an investment in your future. If you need to borrow money to get one, the interest on the loan is a part of the investment. Student loans allow you to postpone repayment until you're out of school and in a job. At the same time, a loan is a loan. If you run up a big bill, you'll be paying for it long after you've forgotten how much fun those all-night study sessions were.

Real estate. The right piece of property in the right location for the right price will go up in value even after interest and inflation. Real estate investments generally require a hefty down payment, a large and steady monthly income, and several years to appreciate significantly—all factors that make it difficult for teenagers to invest.

Borrowing Money from Family and Friends

If you borrow any amount of money, whether it's $5 or $5,000, give the lender an IOU note showing how much you borrowed, when you borrowed it, the amount of the interest, if any, and when he can expect to be paid back. Write out a copy for yourself and put the payback date on your calendar. If you can't pay back on the date you promised, tell the person *beforehand*—don't put him in the uncomfortable position of having to ask you for his own money.

Installment Loans

An installment loan is one that you pay off in a series of payments rather than all at once. It's also called an *amortized* loan. Figuring out the interest on an installment loan is a bit confusing. With a normal loan of $100 at 15 percent interest for one year, you give back the $100 and pay $15 in simple interest at the end of the year.

But with an installment loan, you'd pay only $8.31 in interest. That's because you had their $100 only for the first month. Each month you gave a little bit of it back, and you

THE MEDIAN HOME PRICE IN THE U.S. IN EARLY 1990: $93,100.

paid interest each month only on the amount you owed for that month.

In other words, a twelve-month installment loan is really like *twelve loans*. Let's say you buy a $500 TV with $50 of your own money and finance the rest with the appliance store at 18 percent annual interest. (You've really borrowed $450 from a finance company that works with the store. It bought your TV for you by giving the store $450 in cash. Now you have to pay back the finance company.)

The first month's loan is for $450 at 1.5 percent interest (one-twelfth of 18 percent). You owe $6.75 in interest. If you send a check for $456.75, you'll be completely paid up. Unfortunately, you don't have that much.

All you can afford is $41.25, so you send that much. The

finance company uses $6.75 to pay your interest and applies the rest—$34.50—to pay off your $450 debt. Now you owe $415.50, which the company is willing to loan to you for the next month at 1.5 percent interest.

At the end of the month you owe $6.23 in interest ($415.50 × 1.5 percent). You send another check for $41.25: $6.23 for the interest and $35.02 to help pay off the debt. Now you owe $380.48, which the company loans to you for *another* month at 1.5 percent interest.

As long as you don't pay off the loan the company just extends it for another month at 1.5 percent interest. If you continue to pay $41.25 a month, you will take twelve months to pay it off.

The rule with installment loans is, the larger your payment, the quicker you pay off the loan, and the less interest you pay.

Here's a $5,000 car loan at 12 percent annual interest:

paid off in . . .	monthly payment	total you pay
1 year	$444	$5,331
2 years	235	5,650
5 years	111	6,678

With a five-year loan, you pay $1,678 in interest!

Here's a $100,000 home loan at 10 percent annual interest:

paid off in . . .	monthly payment	total you pay
1 year	$8,792	$105,499
10 years	1,322	158,539
30 years	879	315,307

For a thirty-year loan, you end up paying over three times the original value of the house!

Loan Agreements

If you're under eighteen, lenders won't let you borrow their money unless you have an adult cosigner. Whether you have a cosigner or not, never sign a loan agreement until you've taken it home to study the terms carefully. The agreement, or "note," will list the *principal* (the amount of money you're borrowing), *finance charge* (the interest), *other charges* (late payment fee, early repayment penalty, etc.), *payment information* (the amount, the due dates, where to send them), and *total of payments* (how much you will really pay them by the time the loan is through).

If you end up getting a loan, make the payments on time. If your payment is late, the lender will usually report this to a credit bureau: everyone looking at your credit report will

know. If you mess up two or three times in one year, it looks really bad.

If the loan has no early repayment penalty (can you believe you'd get in trouble for paying back someone too *soon*?), pay it off as rapidly as possible. Even if you add an extra $10 to each payment, you'll pay it off much faster and save interest. If you have money sitting in a bank account and you don't need it for a couple of years, use it to pay off the loan. Then deposit your monthly loan payment into your bank account instead. You'll be the one earning interest on the payments instead of the lender.

16

SETTING AN ALL-TIME CREDIT RECORD

Your credit record is your financial reputation. If you want to rent an apartment, buy a house, have a phone hooked up, get a credit card, take out a loan, buy a blimp, or start a business, you need a good record.

A company that wants to check your credit can call other companies that have done money deals with you in the past, or the firm can get a report from a credit reporting bureau. But if you've never been granted credit in the past, you don't *have* a credit record. Where do you start?

Fortunately, you don't always need a credit record. Some credit grantors realize that no record is better than a bad one. If you don't have one, they'll look more carefully at other information on your credit application:

Income. The longer you hold a job, the better you look. Don't lie about your salary or how long you've worked there; they may call your boss to verify the numbers. If you have other sources of income—side jobs, allowance, whatever—be sure to list these, too. Every little bit helps. Save your check stubs. If someone pays you in cash, make out a "bill," mark it paid, and have her sign it. Make sure that the money you earn can be used to prove your ability to earn more of it.

Your credit record is your financial reputation.

Expenses. You may be asked to list some of your regular expenses such as rent and car insurance. If they don't ask, don't volunteer it; and if they do, list only what is asked for.

Assets. List the amount of money you have in savings and checking accounts (they'll call to verify these, too, so shoot straight). If you have money invested in mutual funds, CDs, or pork belly futures, write it down. Be ready to provide the name of the firm that handled these investments for you. These things suggest that you know how to handle your money. You may wish to mention any toys or vehicles you own that are worth several hundred dollars or more: an expensive camera, a motorcycle, a car, a Bell Jet Ranger helicopter.

Liabilities. If you have any debts—auto or personal loans, charge cards—you'll be asked to list your monthly payment and the outstanding balance (the total you owe).

I'M SORRY, SON, BUT WE DONT THINK YOU COULD PAY OFF THESE DEBTS IF YOU LIVED TO BE A HUNDRED.

If your monthly expenses all but wipe out your income, they'll figure you don't have enough left over to make monthly payments on a loan or credit card debt. If your liabilities (what you *owe*) greatly exceed your assets (what you *own*), they don't want to help you dig your grave deeper. (Actually, they know that once you're in the grave, you won't leave enough behind to pay off the debt.)

But if you have a healthy cash flow, low or no debt, and evidence of good money management habits, you're their kind of customer.

Steps to Build Credit

1. If you're eighteen or older, apply for a credit card from Montgomery Ward or another large department store. These are typically the easiest to qualify for.

2. When you get the card, use it to make one small purchase each month for six months. Make sure it's something you would have bought that month anyway, or charge something your parents need and have them reimburse you for it.

3. Pay your balance in full the moment you get the bill. If you bounce a check or make a late payment, you'll defeat your purpose. By paying the balance in full you avoid paying interest on the "loan," which wastes your money.

4. Each month your payment record is sent to the credit bureau. The people at the bureau will begin a credit record on you, which will be spotless due to your outstanding payment habits.

5. Apply for your next charge card. If your application is accepted, you may wish to close your first card's account by cutting the card in half.

CREDIT REPORTS

Three major companies in the U.S. make a business out of keeping track of your credit history: TRW, Trans Union, and Credit Bureau, Inc. A bank, a credit card issuer, or an employer that wants to know how well you pay your bills usually gets a report from one of these companies. Until you have a credit card, get some kind of loan, or have an overdue bill that goes into collection, you don't have a credit record in their files.

Who Looks at the Report?

Credit card issuers, potential employers, landlords, loan officers, and managers of store credit departments.

What's on the Report?

Credit card and loan accounts for the past seven years. Details include credit limit or amount of the original loan, amount owed, monthly payment, every late payment in the past twenty-four months, whether you paid off the loan or defaulted. As long as you pay all debts "according to terms"— no late payments, bounced checks, overdue balances—you have a perfect payment record. Even if you choose to pay off your VISA card debt over a few months and incur the interest charges, your payments are still "according to terms" so there are no bad marks. If you've been naughty, it stays on your record up to seven years.

Judgments and liens. If the court fines you or someone sues you and you have to pay, a record of it goes on your report.

Bankruptcy. This stays on for ten years.

Inquiries. Every time a company runs a credit check on you, its name and the purpose of the inquiry (auto loan, credit card) goes into the report. If you're applying for credit all over town, it's obvious to those doing the checking.

What's NOT on the Report

Utility bill information (phone, electricity, etc.). But if the payment is so overdue that the utility sends it to a collection agency, that agency may report the debt to the credit bureau.

Savings and checking account activity. Overdrawing your checking account won't put a mark on your credit record. Nor will bouncing a check, unless it was a check to pay a loan or credit card bill, in which case the recipient will tell on you. (If you mess up on a car or personal loan from the bank, you'll be reported.)

What you purchased with your credit card. People looking at your report will be able to tell that you spend $100 every month on your VISA card, but they won't know that you spend it at Toys "R" Us.

How to Look at Your Credit Report

Credit bureaus will send you a copy of your credit report for a small fee, typically $5 to $10. If you've been turned down for credit in the past thirty days because of what someone found on your credit report, you can have the report sent for free. The credit issuer (bank, credit card company) must tell you why you were turned down and the name of the credit bureau it got your report from.

Since you have to request your report in writing, you should call the credit bureau first to learn what to send. You can find the number in the Yellow Pages under Credit Reporting Agencies.

Note: Credit reports can have errors. Sometimes the information was recorded incorrectly, or your parents' or sister's account ends up on your report. If you can prove the error, the bureau is required to fix it.

THE U.S. STOPPED MAKING DIMES AND QUARTERS OUT OF SILVER IN 1965.

17

CARE AND FEEDING OF CREDIT CARDS

Credit cards are convenient but deadly money tools. They can save you in an emergency; they can also put you into deep and lasting debt. In 1989 there were about 795 million credit cards in circulation in the U.S. The average consumer was $1,100 in debt on his credit cards, which included 3 retail cards (e.g., department store cards), 2 bank cards (e.g., VISA, MasterCard), and 1 oil card (e.g., Shell, Texaco).[10]

This chapter will help you understand the different kinds of credit cards, explain how to apply for them, and offer tips to keep you out of trouble with your "plastic."

Minor Note

Most issuers won't give you an account if you're under eighteen. The court won't enforce a contract made with a minor, so if you refuse to pay, the issuer has to eat the loss. A way around the minimum age requirement is to have a parent apply for a card and let you be a cosigner on the account.

Bank Cards

Many banks issue credit cards under the trade names VISA and MasterCard. Charges made with the card are tracked by a computer, which prints and mails a bill for each month that you use the card. The bank that issues you the card usually charges an annual membership fee of $18 to $75. Some banks waive the fee for the first year to entice you to apply. Other banks don't charge a fee at all, charging higher interest rates instead.

With most bank cards, you don't pay any finance charge (interest) as long as you pay your bill in full within the "grace period"—typically 25 days starting the day they mail your bill. But if you pay only a portion of your balance, they'll charge you interest on the unpaid amount (typically around 1.65 percent per month, 19.8 percent annually). Some banks give no grace period; you're charged interest from the day you made the purchase.

To apply for a VISA or MasterCard, you fill out a form that asks you to list your employment history, other sources of income, debts, savings and checking accounts, and other investments. You can get an application by visiting a local bank or savings and loan or by calling or writing for an application with one of the major issuing institutions, such as Bank-America, Citicorp, Chase Manhattan, First Chicago, and AT&T.

It's wise to shop around for the best deal. In most states, issuers can charge whatever annual fees and interest rates they think people are willing to pay. The issuer has to print the interest rate, grace period, membership fee, and other fees on the application. Above all, make sure the card has a twenty-five-day grace period. Cards that charge you interest from the moment you make the purchase are rip-offs.

If you're eighteen and responsible, and you have a reliable income, you should be able to get a card with an $18 annual fee, 19.8 percent annual interest, twenty-five-day grace period, and at least a $500 credit limit.

Other cards: Sears issues a card called Discover; American Express has one called Optima. Their terms are similar, but they're not as widely accepted as VISA and MasterCard.

Travel and Entertainment Cards

American Express and Diners Club are called travel and entertainment (T&E) cards because they've long been used by businesspeople to cover and track business expenses on the road. They work like bank cards, but you have to pay your balance in full every month. Since they don't make money from you in interest charges, they charge higher annual membership fees.

Their biggest advantage is that they make you pay off the balance each month, so there's less temptation to *play now, pay later*. You still get free use of their money from the time you make the charge to the time you have to pay it. This can be up to 55 days, assuming you made the charge on the first day of the 30-day billing cycle and paid your bill on the last day of the 25-day grace period. There's also no credit limit— as long as you've shown an ability to pay in the past. The greatest disadvantage is that they're not accepted in nearly as many places as VISA or MasterCard.

American Express and Diners Club applications can be found in displays at restaurants and stores that accept those cards. Like bank cards, they require that you be at least eighteen and have a verifiable income and a clean credit record. Diners Club also has a minimum income requirement of $25,000, which is tough to earn on minimum wage.

Retail Cards

Lots of department and clothing stores issue charge cards. These behave just like bank cards, complete with grace periods, finance charges, and late fees (but no membership fee). You can pick up an application at a sales counter and often get your card approved while you shop.

To be honest, the best reason to get a retail card is to estab-

lish credit that can help you qualify for a bank or T&E card. Once you've got the bigger card, cut your retail cards in half. (For more on this, see chapter 16.)

Oil Cards

Major oil companies such as Shell, Texaco, and Amoco issue credit cards that can be used at their gas stations. Some of the cards are a cross between a bank card and a T&E card. For any purchases under $50 (e.g., filling up your car), you have to pay your balance in full each month. But if a charge comes to more than $50 (a set of tires, a new engine), you can make partial payments and pay a finance charge as you would with a bank card. An oil card is nice to have when you're driving a very long distance and don't want to carry a

THERE ARE 600 BILLION UNREDEEMED MILES IN FREQUENT-FLYER ACCOUNTS.

load of gas money with you. But if you pay for gas with a card, many stations will charge you more per gallon. Also, the only station that accepts your credit card may be the most expensive in town—or closed when your gauge reads empty.

HOW TO SURVIVE
YOUR CREDIT CARD

Many people become slaves to their credit card debt, living today on money they won't even earn for months to come. Here's how to stay free:

Keep the card in your wallet. It sounds silly, but the best way to control your credit card is to not let it out of your wallet. Paying by card is so painless that you can end up buying things that you can't afford or don't need. Use your credit card only in genuine emergencies or in situations where carrying that much cash is dangerous.

Forget about cash advances. This is one of the most expensive ways to borrow money (loansharks excepted). Never use your bank card for a cash advance or use the checks the bank sends you that get charged to your account. If you do, you'll be charged a fee for the transaction plus very high interest for every day you have the money—there's no grace period.

Beware credit card companies that automatically send you a cash advance when your application is accepted. They're hoping you'll give in and spend the money instead of returning the check. When you're unable to pay back all the money on the first bill, you'll choose to make the recommended partial payment instead. A few months of partial payments, and they've got you hooked into a habit.

Flee from fees. There are fees for getting cash advances,

using credit card checks, making late payments, going over your limit, and paying with a bad check. These and any others are listed in your agreement—learn them and avoid them.

TAKE YOUR TIME, ENJOY THE CARD, LIVE A LITTLE!

Pay in full. Bank and retail card issuers make most of their money from finance charges—interest on unpaid balances. When it comes to paying your bills, they want you to "take your time." Don't give in. Pay every bill in full within the grace period. The safest way is to pay the bill the day you receive it.

If you want to get full use of their money without paying interest, pay the bill seven days before the grace period expires. Put that date in your calendar—and keep your appointment. A late payment hurts you in three ways: an interest charge on the unpaid balance, a late fee, and a late payment mark on your credit record.

If they're selling it, you don't need it. You'll be bombarded with "statement stuffers" and junk mail offering you credit card insurance, medical coverage, travel clubs, stereos, and microwaves—all of which can be yours for just a few dollars a month, conveniently added to your bill. Throw the offers away. You probably don't need the stuff—and if you do, you'll get a much better deal shopping elsewhere.

Keep in touch. If you're going to be late paying a bill, or you've misplaced it, call the phone number listed on your statements; it's usually toll free. Look at it from the company's perspective. If someone owed you money but was going to have a problem paying you back, wouldn't you rather have him tell you about it beforehand instead of waiting and wondering if he's moved to Mongolia? Another thing: if you disagree with a charge on your bill, call and discuss it. Not paying it will just cost you interest and possibly get you a bad credit rating.

18

HOW TO SPEND MONEY

Many people have a simple money management philosophy: if I have it, I spend it till I don't have it.

Others are so good with money it makes you sick. These are the ones who save every penny they've ever found, then buy a new Porsche on their sixteenth birthday.

Assuming you didn't trade your pennies for a Porsche, here are some tips to help you spend less and get more for your money. Also, there are some suggestions for buying a car and deciding what to do when a friend wants to borrow money.

Spending Less

Most of us don't seem to have any problem spending money; our problem is learning not to spend it! I've discovered some sales "defense" tactics:

• *Ask why*. Ask yourself, Why do I want to buy this thing? It's amazing how silly some of your purchases look when you ask that question.

• *Count to seven*. Live by the seven over seven rule. Anytime you want to buy something that costs over $7, you have to wait seven days. This will blow a big hole in your impulse buying habits!

• *Don't "save" money by spending it.* Walk away when someone says a deal is "too good to pass up" or "you'll never find as good a deal as this one." You'll always find a better deal. For example, keeping your money in savings is a better deal. Don't let salespeople pressure you into making decisions "before it's too late." If you shop around, you'll usually find something as good or better—or discover you didn't need the thing after all.

• *Hang around people who spend less.* If the main pastime of your group of friends is shopping, chances are that you're going to spend more money than you should.

• *Write it down.* Every time you spend money write down what you bought and how much you paid. Buying something isn't as easy when you have to find your expense book and write down the transaction. Hold a contest with yourself to see how little money you can live on each week. Set goals and reward yourself when you meet them.

• *Get some advisers.* Invite two good friends with smart money habits to be your financial advisers. Whenever you want to spend more than $20 on something, you must present the idea to them and receive their unanimous approval. If they object, you can't buy it.

• *Keep extra cash at home.* Each morning put in your wallet only the amount of money you know you'll need for that day's essentials.

Saving More

Instead of buying things that go down in value, save your money and let it work for you. (For more ideas, see chapter 14.)

• *Empty your pockets.* At the end of each day, dump all your pocket change in a jar. Empty the jar every month and deposit the coins in the bank. It seems like a small amount of money, but it adds up over a few months into some real cash.

• *Buy off a bad habit.* If you smoke, eat junk foods, or drink twelve Diet Cokes a day, give it up. Figure out how much money you spend on your habit, then put that money in the bank instead.

• *Use direct deposit.* Some employers can deposit your paycheck directly into your savings account.

• *Go through withdrawal pains.* If you have a problem keeping your savings in the bank where it belongs, set up an account that requires two signatures for a withdrawal—yours and a parent's.

Buying a Car

Some facts on car buying:

• The third most expensive way to buy a car: borrow money to pay for it.

• The second most expensive way to buy a car: insist on buying a new car.

• The most expensive way to buy a car: borrow money to buy a new one.

If you want to get the best possible deal on a car, consider the following ideas:

• *Let someone else pay for the new-car smell.* "New" is an expensive taste. A new car's value can drop by as much as 40 percent in the first two years.[11] Look for a good used car instead.

• *Watch for warranties.* Because most new cars come with warranties that last from two to six years, you may be able to buy a used car with a few years left on the warranty.

• *Look for cars that are slow on the downhill.* Most cars go down in value once you buy them—but some go downhill faster than others. Shop for a car that has a history of slow depreciation. Near the top of the list, Toyota Corollas and Honda Accords lose about 33 percent of their new car value in five years; the worst cars lose twice that.[12] Obviously, a car retains its value better when it's well built, looks good, and requires little maintenance. *Consumer Reports* magazine reports on the reliability of used cars in its *Used Car Buying Guide*—look for it at the library.

Lending Money to People You Like

Don't lend money to a friend (or a family member) unless you're ready for the possibility that you'll never get it back. In other words, would you give (not lend) your money to the

person if she needed it that badly? If the answer is yes, go ahead and lend her the money. If she can't repay you, you're no worse off than if you had given the money. If you get your money back, you got an even better deal.

Just the same, it's best to let the person know that you expect the money back. There's a difference between letting a flaky friend off the hook and forgiving the debt of a person who is really struggling to get by. Get your friend to sign an IOU. Here is a sample:

> I, Garth Mashville, agree to repay my dear friend and buddy for life, Steve Lim, every penny of the $555 I borrowed from him on September 6. I further acknowledge his generosity and declare my sworn fealty to him by dismissing any thought of ever stiffing him, nay, never, spit in my eye, hope to die, nuh-uh, I wouldn't do it. No. And if I don't repay him within 60 earth days, I will voluntarily move to Mars.

> Signature _____ Date _____

19

GIVING AWAY YOUR MONEY LIKE AN ABSOLUTE MANIAC

Once upon a time, people gave their time and money to help those less fortunate than themselves. You didn't do it because you felt guilty or because you were told to do so. You did it because it was the right thing to do; anything less just wasn't decent.

Most religions encouraged giving. When Moses led the Jewish people out of slavery in Egypt, they left town with nothing but the clothes on their backs. It was obvious to them that everything they received from that point on was a gift from God: the food they ate, the water they drank—and eventually, the land they settled in. So when they gave away 10 percent of their food and money, they were simply giving back to God what He gave them.

Many Jews and Christians continue to follow this tradition. They don't give a percentage of their money to God; they give *back* a portion of what He gave to them in the first place.

But somewhere along the way, people stopped giving. For most of us, providing for the needy isn't our "problem" anymore. It's the government's job. And when the government doesn't provide food, shelter, jobs, or medical care, we declare it heartless and unfair. But the government's conscience is just an unflattering reflection of its people's. How can we expect the government to be more giving than its citizens?

I think that if your only giving is in the form of taxes, you're missing out on a thrilling and powerful way to spend your money.

What Happens When You Give on Your Own

You help the people you want. Congress decides where your tax dollars go. So the money often goes to the agencies with the right political connections or the most media coverage. By giving on your own, you ensure the survival and growth of private agencies that may not get government funds and those without headline-grabbing missions.

You have fun. You may want to give for the fun of it. If you like Christmas because you enjoy watching your family open gifts you've made or bought for them, why wait all year to feel that thrill? Giving a portion of your income each month spreads the Christmas spirit all over the calendar.

You feel significant. There are over 5 billion people on this planet, and something inside drives us to be more than a number in the world census. We want our lives to count for something. If you give $21 each month to sponsor a child in another country, you're paying for his food, clothing, and education. You may not know the square root of 225 or how to spell Albuquerque (or is it Albakurkey?), and you may not be able to do five pull-ups or empty the trash without being reminded; but you're risking your money to keep someone else alive—and that's at least a trillion times more impressive than good spelling.

You set people free. When you give to organizations that help the needy, you're enabling others to experience the freedom you enjoy. Most people in this world are trapped by something they can't free themselves from: hunger, disease, thirst, poverty, war, handicapping condition. People want to taste freedom—giving makes that possible.

You say thanks to God. If you believe that God is the ultimate provider of things, giving to others is one way you can thank Him for the opportunity to use His money to meet your needs and desires. Many people take one-tenth of what they have and set it to work to express thanks for the nine-tenths they have the privilege of using. Other people give more than that—some nearly everything they have. (This percentage giving is also called tithing, from an Old English word meaning "tenth.") The joy of giving is a thrilling act of faith.

ADULT ADMISSION TO DISNEYLAND: $27.50.

Appearance of Guilt

Okay, it's true. One reason I give is that I feel guilty. I look at what I'm wearing:

Reebok shoes	$ 70
socks	5
Levi's	25
Superman underwear	5
cotton shirt	20
jacket	75
Casio watch	80
leather wallet	20
TOTAL	$300

The average person in Haiti makes $300 per *year*. Something inside me declares foul. It's not my mind. My mind is saying, "The cost of living is lower in Haiti, so $300 goes much further there." My mind also points out to me: "You dress like a slob—you don't *deserve* to feel guilty until you've got some jewelry, designer labels, and a Rolex." But my heart still tells me that despite all logic, there's something wrong with my always wanting more without considering those who have less. So I give, and it makes me appreciate the incredible riches I have and think less about the silly things I don't have hanging in my closet.

How to Give Away Your Money

Lots of people give money every once in a while—usually when someone asks for it. But the real power in giving comes when you give every month to the same causes. The best kind of giving adds up, little by little, month to month, year to year, like a savings account. But with giving, you're saving more than money. If you'd like to give a portion of your income regularly, here are some steps to get you started:

1. Pick a percentage. Choose a percentage of your income that you'd like to give each month. Do a budget to make sure that you can afford the amount you commit to. Keep a record of all your income each month so you'll know how much to base your percentage on.

2. Choose a day. Decide which day of the month you plan to do your giving. Mark it in your calendar.

IN 1988, INDIVIDUALS IN THE U.S. GAVE $86.7 BILLION.

3. Decide who you want to give to. Keep your eyes open, and ask around. Needs aren't hard to find. Do some homework to make sure the organizations are legitimate—doing what they say they're doing with your money.

4. Commit to giving a certain amount each month for one year. Take an average of your last few months' incomes and multiply this by your giving percentage: that's how much you can commit every month. It's smart to leave yourself a little pad in case you bring in less money some months. After you've given to your regular commitments, put the leftover in your bank account and record it on a "leftover sheet." If your income dips for a month and you don't have enough to cover your commitments, you can make up the difference with the leftover fund. If that fund gets big, you can make a one-time gift to something special.

5. Team up. Don't be afraid to team up with friends so that your giving has greater impact. Four students who can't individually afford to sponsor needy children in other countries can join forces—each chipping in $5.25 every month to sponsor one child.

6. Graduate. Every year, try to add a point to your giving percentage. If you give 5 percent this year, give 6 percent starting next year. You'll hardly notice the increase, but it will make a difference in your giving over time. Assuming you make $4 per hour and average eighty hours per month, your gross pay (i.e., before taxes) is $320 per month. Giving 5 percent means $16; 6 percent is $19.20. But after a year of giving, the higher percentage will mean $230 instead of $192.

Imagine this. You're sixteen, and you decide to give 5 percent of your income this year and add 1 percent each year. Assume you work about eighty hours per month (more in the summer, less during the school year), and you get raises every year.

your age	hourly wage	annual gross income	giving rate	total given
16	$4.50	$4,320	5%	$ 216
17	5.00	4,800	6%	288
18	5.50	5,280	7%	370
19	6.00	5,760	8%	461
20	6.50	6,240	9%	562

FIVE-YEAR TOTAL $1,897

That's almost $2,000 in five years. If you were really bold, you'd start at 10 percent at age sixteen, and work up to 14

percent by age twenty. Assuming the same raises, your giving would look like this:

your age	hourly wage	annual gross income	giving rate	total given
16	$4.50	$4,320	10%	$ 432
17	5.00	4,800	11%	528
18	5.50	5,280	12%	634
19	6.00	5,760	13%	749
20	6.50	6,240	14%	874

FIVE-YEAR TOTAL $3,217

The point is that if you start your percentage giving now and increase your percentage annually as your income increases, your giving will never be a great burden to you.

Giving: A Sure Thing

Looking at the total amount of money you'd be giving away makes you think, *Wow, what I could buy with that money if I didn't give it away.* But if you try it, you'll discover something really crazy. If you spend the money on yourself, it may make you happier, and it may not. But if you give it away, the joy you get is a sure thing. But the truth of this bizarre phenomenon is known only to those who are crazy enough to try it.

20

WHEN YOU CAN'T BUY WHAT YOU WANT

I know a man whose monthly house payment was $30,000. Working 22 weekdays a month, he had to earn $136 *every hour* of a ten-hour day. Of course, he had to earn over twice that much to pay for his family's cars, boats, vacations, clothes, insurance, food, and orthodontist bills.

I know a woman who spends at least $20,000 every month on clothes and jewelry. It's worse around Christmas.

I know a man in Haiti who earns about $300 per year to support his family of six. They live in a mud-and-reed hut: dirt floor, no water, no heat, no electricity.

All of these people have something in common: they can't afford what they want.

The first man struggled to make his house payment—some months he fell behind. I know what you're thinking: Why didn't he sell his $3 million home and settle for something he could afford . . . like a $2 million home? But in his world, that would be an embarrassing step backward. Kind of like if you and your friends all drove beautiful new cars, but you had to sell yours and buy a clunky used one.

The woman struggles to pay her credit card bills every month, but she carries a $10,000 unpaid balance. There never seems to be enough money in her checking account to pay it off completely, so she pays an extra $150 in finance charges each month. Sure, she could try to limit her fashion purchases to just $15,000 a month, but there's always some new occasion that demands another $5,000 dress: a party, a dinner in Rome, a night at the ballet. (Would you wear the same dress to every formal occasion?)

And my friend in Haiti struggles to stretch his income. He would like a wood house, better education for his sons, and a mule, but he always runs out of money before he runs out of needs.

It's a fact. You'll never be able to afford what you want. The

reason has something to do with materialism. Materialism is the tendency to put more value on physical things than on spiritual or intellectual things. Like when you eat, make money, or buy things just to bring you happiness.

The problem with materialism is that the happiness it delivers is never quite enough to fill your need. So you keep buying, eating, drinking, sleeping around, or whatever. But you never feel satisfied.

A popular form of materialism is consumerism, whose followers play by the rule, "Whoever dies with the most toys wins." To play, you keep buying toys and clothes and stereos and cds and shoes and electronic gadgets and cars and anything else you think will give you pleasure, until you run out of money—or die.

Unfortunately, the companies that sell these things tell you that their products will bring you the very things you feel you're missing on the inside: jeans that make every guy stop and pay attention, a car that identifies you as the cool person you want to be, shoes that let you fit in with the right crowd, high-performance toys that announce to the world that you know how to have fun. But if you've played this game at all, you know that the promises of the advertisers are mostly empty.

You know the feeling. You've felt the thrill of buying some really great stuff with your money only to have that thrill shrink to a sense of profound emptiness when the stuff doesn't satisfy the void inside. It's more than buyer's remorse; it's a deep longing for something you can't buy.

If the material world cannot fill the need in your heart, there are two possibilities: either life is a cruel joke—a frustrating and pointless search for satisfaction you can never have—or

"WHOEVER LOVES MONEY NEVER HAS MONEY ENOUGH; WHOEVER LOVES WEALTH IS NEVER SATISFIED WITH HIS INCOME."—Solomon

it's time to discover that there's a spiritual side to you that, having been created by God, will never be satisfied until you're connected with Him.

A few years ago Madonna told us that we live in a material world. But another song, by Sting, declared the truth: "We are spirits in the material world . . . there must be another way."

THEN THERE ARE SOME NOTES

1. U.S. Census, 1950, 1960.
2. Rand Youth Poll, New York; as reported in *The Wall Street Journal,* May 3, 1990, p. A1.
3. Teen Research Unlimited, Northbrook, Ill.; as reported in *The Wall Street Journal,* February 2, 1990, p. B1.
4. Michele Manges, "The Dead-End Kids," *The Wall Street Journal,* February 9, 1990, p. R36.
5. Mike Vance, *Creative Thinking* (Chicago, Nightingale Conant Corp., 1982), audio session 2.
6. Brian Bremmer: "Among Restaurateurs, It's Dog Eat Dog"; *Business Week,* January 9, 1989, p. 86.
7. Michele Manges, "The Dead End Kids."
8. Joyce Lain Kennedy and Dr. Darryl Laramore, *Joyce Lain Kennedy's Career Book* (Chicago: National Textbook Company, 1988), p. 236.
9. Ibid., p. 241.
10. *U.S. News & World Report,* April 9, 1990, p. 21.
11. Ibid., p. 62.
12. Ibid.

Margin Facts Sources

Business Week.
The Inc. Life.

U.S. News & World Report.

The Wall Street Journal.

The Wall Street Journal Guide to Understanding Money & Markets, Richard Saul Wurman, Alan Siegel, Kenneth M. Morris, (New York: Prentice Hall, 1989).

The World Almanac and Book of Facts 1990 (New York: Pharos Books, 1989).